True life experiences of awakening, revelation and transformation

Out Of The Blue

Jesus, Self-Realization, Death & Creation

....and God spoke, "Here is your Divinity,
the Divinity that awaits all Mankind."

Mary Terhune, RN

Grateful acknowledgment is made for permission to reprint the following copyrighted material:

"The Odes of Solomon" (p.24) from THE ENLIGHTENED HEART: AN ANTHOLOGY OF SACRED POETRY, EDITED BY STEPHEN MITCHELL
Copyright © 1989 by Stephen Mitchell.
Reprinted by permission of HarperCollins Publishers

© Cover page and back page photograph|Ron Chapple|Agency: Dreamstime.com

© Photograph of leaf on page 110|Joanne Shapiro

OUT OF THE BLUE, Jesus, Self-Realization, Death & Creation
ISBN: 978-0-6151-4318-7

First published in 2007 by Terhune Press, 1 Columbia Street, P.O. Box 864, Ayer, MA 01432

Manufacturing by Lulu Enterprises, Inc.
Morrisville, NC 27560
http://www.lulu.com

This Book's Lulu Web Page:
http://www.lulu.com/content/605732

For more information on the author, visit:
http://www.ournaturaldestiny.com

For my grandson Nicolas

When Nicolas was three months old.
he came to me in a dream and said,

"God is consciousness,
I am consciousness,
Everything is consciousness,
The people need to know.
I'm glad you're here
with me Mary,
I like the name Mary."

For my grandchildren
Ryan, Leigh, Paul and Joseph,
my daughters Deborah and Cindy,
and all children whose faces
shine with the Light of God.

OUT OF THE BLUE
Jesus, Self-Realization, Death & Creation

CONTENTS

Introduction

The time has come for all of us to experience the Truth of Divinity within ourselves and within each other. It is a Truth that lives in all religions but does not belong to any religion. It can be called spirituality, the life of the Spirit. It is said that a spark of the Sun is still the Sun. In the same way a spark of God is still God. And so it is with us. It is an exciting time to be alive now, as the consciousness of humanity awakens to itself on the world stage.

The veil is beginning to slip between the ego, our lower consciousness, and the Truth of who we really are, Divine consciousness. To be identified with the ego keeps us bound in a state of mind called suffering, with its emotional companions of fear, separation, anger, loneliness and lack. Divine consciousness brings us to the realm of our natural state of mind, that of being identified as God, also known as Self-Realization. It is a state of mind filled with peace, bliss and all-knowing.

We are here on this Earth to wake up to that which we already are: Self-Realized beings, God in action. The sages call it being a *jivanmukta,* one who is liberated while living in the body. Liberated from what? Liberated from the identification of ourselves as the body, when in Truth we are the Light of God.

We are using the body for an earthly experience, only to rediscover our true Self, our Divine consciousness housed in the body. This consciousness is the energy that gives life to the body and allows the mind to think. When this consciousness leaves the body, we call it death. In reality, neither birth nor death truly exist.

My own journey of spiritual awakening began over twenty years ago and has continued to this day. The opening began with an experience of the Master Jesus. Although I was brought up in the Catholic tradition, the Jesus I experienced with this awakening was free from any religious dogma or fanaticism. He did not belong to any particular country or religion and yet belonged to all countries and all religions. I believe this is true of all Self-Realized beings. I believe this is true of us as well.

I am sharing my experiences of Self-Realization, death and creation because they are universal experiences available to everyone. I hope my shared experiences and realizations bring comfort, affirmation and inspiration to those reading this book. You may recognize some of them as your own, while others may be surprising. Either way, they will feel familiar, as the Truth lives in all of us and these experiences will have the ring of Truth.

I hope this book is helpful, as eventually, in this lifetime or next, the awakening of the Soul happens to everyone. Self-Realization is our birthright and our natural destiny; its natural consequence is freedom from the fear of death and suffering. The purpose of Self-Realization is to bring forth our true nature and from that vantage point, to serve the world.

In this inner terrain of Self-Realization rests solutions, understandings and knowledge with which to assist humanity in our many fields of endeavor, including our educational, medical, financial, environmental, social and political systems. The greatness within ourselves will be experienced on a global level. Divinity is our destiny and the time for this knowledge and experience of it as a living reality has arrived.

Territories of Divine consciousness already existing within ourselves are to be fully awakened creating new conversations and possibilities. May our new conversations include everyone. May our new conversations support everyone. May we become love in action. This is what happened to me.

Chapter 1

AWAKENING

It was a Saturday in May, and my daughter Deborah was away visiting her father. I was sitting on the couch in my living room berating myself, consumed with anxiety. This day was a culmination of a lifetime of bad feelings. A feeling of deep despair came over me. I wondered how I would survive physically and emotionally. I felt like a complete loser. My current life situation involved the loss of my life savings in a recent real estate deal gone bad. What made it worse was friends were involved and I neglected to hire my own real estate agent or lawyer. I was at the lowest point of my life. The difficulty of my life overwhelmed me and I felt I could not escape from it.

My mind searched for answers, but could find none. I felt weighed down by all my thoughts. How could I have been so stupid to allow myself to lose my investment in the house? Now I was in deep debt with nowhere to turn. I had been so affected by these events, that I was on the brink of losing my job. I was unable to shake a feeling of doom. At some point my mind could no longer think and I gave up. I just surrendered everything to my misery.

Having reached the end of all hope, finding myself on the brink of emotional collapse, I put my head in my hands and began to sob uncontrollably, deeper than I ever thought possible. I felt all the losses and disappointments throughout my life. In essence, my life felt like one long burdensome event after another. Why did happiness seem so elusive? Would this be the way I would go throughout life? Was that all there was for me? Had this been pre-ordained? I once heard someone say, when you cry, you don't cry for just one thing, you cry for everything. And this everything I called my life was filled with overwhelming sadness, failures and confusion.

My sobs turned into wailing from the depths of my soul, as the story of my life played out like a movie onto the screen of my mind. On the screen, I saw myself as a young child, so delighted with life, nature and animals, and then my family fell apart after my mother left. I felt the devastation of it more deeply than ever. I felt totally abandoned and unloved. Then I saw myself as a young teen, lost and angry, and at the age of nineteen, pregnant with a child I was forced to give up for adoption. The picture moved to my marriage in my late twenties, which resulted in the birth of my younger daughter and which ended in divorce. I saw myself seeking refuge in relationships trying to get from them what I felt I lacked. This left me feeling helpless and incomplete. The picture fast-forwarded to my present circumstance, in which I had lost all the money I had worked so hard for over the years. I felt all was lost and could not be fixed. I felt my life was laying at my feet in total ruin.

I sobbed until I thought I would die. The pain became so unbearable that I found myself calling out to a God I had long felt deserted me, to a God I was sure did not exist. "Please God, just let me die, let me die. It's too painful, it's too hard."

I felt myself falling off a cliff into a pitch-black endless abyss. I tumbled further and further and felt there was no bottom to it. I wondered where I was going. I let myself fall. I simply didn't care anymore. I thought about how I had lost everything and about friends who let me down. Why did they do it? As I asked those questions, all of a sudden I started to view my life and myself from the perspective of a compassionate witness. Then, I heard this witness voice say, "This child, teen and adult you condemn could not help these things. She always had a loving heart; she did the best she could given the circumstances. You can't condemn her. She didn't know." These words entered me very deeply and I felt the kind, compassionate energy of them. I felt a wave of self-forgiveness wash over me. I had no idea where it came from.

As I started to forgive myself, simultaneously and automatically, I forgave all those who I felt had offended me throughout my life. I remember feeling my heart release its emotional knots in this forgiveness. I had never really understood how to forgive myself before. But now I was somehow being given the experience of it. The depth of this self-forgiveness was deeper than I ever thought possible. It was as if there was no one to forgive but myself. What a curious and freeing feeling.

I felt so free and light in my body, as if I could almost fly. I then saw pictures in my mind's eye of those who I felt had betrayed me. I saw that they too only did the best they could. They too had lived their lives mostly out of fear and out of the need to survive and to make it in this world. Like me, their actions were driven by fear and from the sense of not having enough.

As this feeling of deep self-forgiveness began to enter my heart, a miraculous event occurred. A great wave of Light began to fill the entire room, quieting my sobs. This Light poured in like an ocean through the front windows of my living room.

I watched in awe from where I was sitting on the couch. Everything felt as if it were moving in slow motion, my mind, my thoughts and my body. The Light was a soft, golden yellow color. It was as if the Sun itself had entered the room washing over everything covering me like a blanket. I felt so peaceful. This force was so strong, I could not sit up anymore and I had to lay down. I felt a deep, loving Presence come over me, soothing every cell in my

3

body and I could not keep my eyes open in its force. What was this force?

In my mind's eye, I saw a manger and the little baby Jesus appear in my heart region. What was this? The familiar Christmas story played out in my mind with the Virgin Mary being refused a room in the Inn and the Jesus child having to be born in a manger. I had a thought, or perhaps I heard a thought, "Are you not like him?" The words echoed in my mind, "Are you not like him? Are you not like him?" The strains of an old familiar gospel song filled my mind, "Sweet little Jesus child, they had you born in a manger, Oh little holy child, they didn't know who you were, didn't know how to ask you Lord to take our sins away, our eyes were blind, we could not see and we didn't know who you were."

I somehow had an immediate understanding from this inner picture that we, each of us, were this little Holy Child, and this Holy Child represented our goodness. It was an innate goodness that we had all but forgotten. I saw how forgetfulness of our true nature kept us acting out of fear—fear of not having enough, fear of not being enough—and I saw how we justified our actions based on this fear.

As I lay on the couch absorbing this golden Light, I reveled in it. I felt as if all my burdens were being lifted and a calmness came over me that was unlike anything I had ever experienced. I became very quiet and still. My breathing slowed down. I felt all the energy centers of my body flowing freely. I felt calm and protected. Then I noticed something strange about my breathing. I didn't seem to be breathing from my lungs. I seemed to be breathing from a space that ran adjacent to my spinal column, deep inside me. I remembered hearing about yogis who could somehow breathe when buried alive. I wondered if this was the deep inner breathing center they were able to access, enabling them to stay alive. As I lay on the couch, feeling peaceful and quiet, I heard a distinct voice, unlike any other I have ever heard, speak to me. Immediately, I knew who it was. It was the Master Jesus.

Chapter 2

Jesus Speaks

THE FIRST REVELATION:
ON FORGIVENESS

I could hardly believe it was Him! His voice felt at once so familiar and so unique. It seemed to hold a feeling in it that I could only equate with the softest, most compassionate love I had ever experienced. He spoke, **"Now do you understand what true forgiveness is?"** As Jesus spoke these words, I was infused with His Divine Light, which contained the full knowledge and wisdom of forgiveness. In familiar computer terms, the information, knowledge and experience of forgiveness were somehow "downloaded" into my being, into all my cells, infusing them with the wisdom and knowledge inherent in His words. It was an instantaneous transfer of information on all levels of my being, in a flash of light, so to speak.

As Jesus spoke the question on forgiveness, the example of my own life stood before me as if on a movie screen. I saw and felt that as I forgave myself as a compassionate witness of my life instead of as a critical judge, my entire being become the embodiment of forgiveness. Blame fled from me in the face of this Divine understanding. I neither blamed myself nor blamed others. I understood that things had to happen in my life the way they happened. There was nothing to change and no one to blame. I felt freer inside. I felt love inside, so free, so pure. I understood that true forgiveness was really self-forgiveness. That was the crux of His teaching. I understood this completely and saw how it applied to my life. The difficult things in my life that happened had to happen. I could not control them and I could not change them at the time they were happening. I had to live them out.

Jesus made the experience of self-forgiveness very clear. He called it "true forgiveness." I had always thought forgiveness was something I did for other people. But on this day, beyond any shadow of a doubt, I knew it as something I did for myself. I had always tried to understand forgiveness on an intellectual level. Jesus gave me the experience of it.

I was grateful for being given this experience. I felt freed from the suffering of having angry thoughts about those who had treated me badly. Now I knew I didn't have to hold on to bad feelings. I understood true forgiveness took great courage. Could I be that courageous? When I understood and experienced all that Jesus had to say on forgiveness, He moved onto another subject: **Judgment**.

Chapter 3

Jesus Speaks

THE SECOND REVELATION: ON JUDGMENT

Jesus spoke again. **"Judge not, fear ye be judged."** As I heard those words, the experience, wisdom and knowledge contained within them infused into my being in the same way as the teaching on forgiveness. Immediately, I had the inner experience and understanding that "Judge not, fear ye be judged" literally meant to judge another was to judge myself right then and there! No waiting. I had always thought the phrase meant don't judge someone for fear they will judge you at some future date. But this was not true. I had the inner experience that all people were alike in some fundamental way and if I judged someone, it would immediately come back to me in an injurious way like a boomerang. This also meant not judging myself. The statement on judgment tied in very beautifully to Jesus' teaching on forgiveness. If I forgave myself and didn't judge myself, then automatically I would forgive and not judge others. It seemed too simple and so obvious. I also realized the Truth is simple but not so obvious.

I was also rather horrified at what Jesus was saying about judgment, as I sifted through the files of my mind to count how many times I had judged another. I looked at what judging was. I saw it as a critical approach when viewing another. Why did I do it? Did I need to feel right because I felt so wrong? Clearly I had a lot of inner work to do to release this automatic mental habit. Why didn't I just see the best in another person instead of their weaknesses? I realized this mental habit very definitely started with how I viewed myself. If I was self-critical and condemned my own weaknesses then this habit of negative thinking spilled out on to the world I viewed every day. I knew it would take a concerted effort on my part to turn the bad habit into a good habit. I needed to develop the habit of seeing the strengths in others. I knew it meant starting to see the strengths in myself. It had to start with self-forgiveness and not judging myself.

When Jesus finished giving me the experience and knowledge of judgment, He moved onto another topic: **the Bible**.

Chapter 4

Jesus Speaks

THE THIRD REVELATION:
ON THE BIBLE

Then Jesus said, **"Now do you see how they misuse my words in the Bible?"** As I heard His words, I simultaneously had the physical, emotional and intellectual understanding of this question and statement. I understood that "Now do you see how they misuse my words in the Bible?" was a statement and question all rolled into one and had many meanings. I was infused with His inner thoughts: "Now do you see how people misuse my words against each other to validate their hatred and judgment? Now do you see how they take my words and use them as weapons to make others feel bad? I never meant for that to happen." As I had heard Jesus' thoughts, I also felt His compassionate love. He understood the human struggle; it was always easier to hate than to love. It was always easier to blame.

I recognized that "they misuse my words in the Bible" also meant that sometimes Jesus was not always understood and, therefore, not quoted correctly. I understood that sometimes the Truth in His words and what Jesus really meant by them had been lost and/or misinterpreted. I felt His profound sadness that this had happened. I understood He never wanted to become a weapon to be used by religions to make people fear Him or God. He never wanted to become the property of a particular religion. I understood that Jesus' words stood on their own. They were not to be held hostage to any particular caste, sect, religion, idea, theory, dogma, nation, country or people. The Truth of His words needed to be experienced and understood inside in the heart and never used in judgment against another.

As I wondered how Humanity had gotten so sidetracked from Jesus' original meanings, Jesus spoke again, this time on: **Weight Problems**.

Chapter 5

Jesus Speaks

THE FOURTH REVELATION:
ON WEIGHT PROBLEMS

Then Jesus said to me **"Now do you see what weight problems are all about?"** As He spoke the words, He also gave me the experience and knowledge of the origins surrounding weight problems. He infused my being with this knowledge and I immediately felt my emotions and thoughts as energies. I saw these energies swirling around my physical body, feeding into it. I started examining my feelings of self-hatred, anger and sadness as energies; they had a certain heaviness to them that hung in my consciousness, blocking the natural flow of light and love within my being. My body then reflected what I was thinking and feeling. These feelings and thoughts were like a bunch of heavy suitcases of accumulated sorrow and disappointment that I carried around in my subtle body of thoughts and emotions. I saw how the weight of my emotions manifested as physical weight in order to bring my attention to unattended feelings and issues.

My own life experience flashed before me. Ever since I started to deal with my old emotional baggage, I started to lose physical weight. As I released the heavy feelings, I felt lighter inside and this was reflected in my physical body.

As I was given the experience and knowledge of these issues surrounding weight, I felt my energy centers, the chakras, open from the top of my head down to the bottom of my spine. I felt the chakras mainly in the front of my body as energy points opening and whirling around. I understood the more I released negative thoughts in my mind and emotions, the more freely these energy centers would spin. I experienced that these energy centers were composed of light and were an extension of the Light of my soul.

I had remembered from my readings, that the main seven chakras were located along the spinal column starting at the top of the head going down to the end of the spine and that each chakra had an endocrine gland associated with it. I knew that the endocrine glands were responsible for the psychological and physiological health of the body.

As I felt these chakras open and spin on the surface of my body, I became increasingly more peaceful and felt a sense of wholeness. I understood that tightly held emotions and negative thoughts impeded the flow in the chakras and therefore impeded the endocrine glands from functioning at their optimal level. Everything that began in my thoughts (mind/consciousness) ended up being expressed in my physical body which included weight. It seemed to me that the more I could release on a mental/emotional level, the healthier I would be on a physical level.

It was incredible to feel this Light energy of my soul consciousness moving freely in my body and I had the direct experience of being able to somehow absorb this Light as nourishment. It was a strange experience. I felt myself breathing in this Light into every cell of my body and I felt so completely full and satisfied on every level.

For weeks after this experience, I needed very little food. What I did eat was rice and vegetables and a little chicken, very simple and pure, which I cooked myself. I never felt very hungry. In fact, I felt as if I fed off the Light as a food, as a nectar. The more I seemed to live in the Light, the more satisfied I felt on every level. I wondered if it could be this way all the time. In the days and weeks that followed, my bodyweight dropped from 119 to 100 pounds. At 5' 3" I was quite slim and felt healthy and very energetic.

I wondered why, of all things that Jesus could talk to me about, he chose weight problems as it related to the energy system of the body. I could only assume it was because I chose to be in the healing profession and would need to understand this, not only for myself, but to share this understanding with others.

When Jesus finished imparting His knowledge about weight problems and the chakras, He moved onto the subject of **Disease**.

Chapter 6

Jesus Speaks

THE FIFTH REVELATION:
ON DISEASE

Then Jesus said, **"Now do you understand what disease is all about?"** As he spoke these words, he gave me the understanding that all diseases in our physical bodies begin first on an energetic level including our emotions and thoughts. Once again I felt the experience of this knowledge inside my own physical and emotional bodies as He "downloaded" His understanding into me. I had a vision of the energies of thoughts and feelings hovering around my physical body feeding their energy into it.

Again I saw the experiences of my own life. Hadn't my migraines been cured as I faced the anger built up from the hurt and sorrow in my childhood? Telling the truth of my life had begun to quite literally set me free. Hadn't my lower back problems all started with deeply held anxieties that so wracked my body that it caused discs to herniate? Hadn't my nervous anxieties and panic attacks all been caused by my inabilities to address and express my deepest emotional wounds? All of these emotional and physical aliments were mere reflections of the "dis-ease" that had first begun in my emotions and thoughts. I understood that being unable to deal with my thoughts and emotions directly and fully at the moment they occurred, I stored the energy of these feelings in my subtle consciousness where they festered. They finally appeared as symptoms in my physical body. I knew all of this was true.

I further understood that I inherited negativities and thought patterns from my family. I realized my mind and emotions played a powerful role in my health and in the types of diseases from which I suffered. I saw how I could affect my health in a positive way, by addressing unresolved mental/emotional issues on the thought/feeling level before they manifested on the physical level in order to get my attention.

I saw that guilt should not play a role when we looked at our health. I understood that we must be completely compassionate with ourselves. I realized that sometimes we were destined to experience disease as a teacher in order to awaken ourselves to inner realities of Divine love.

I realized in the West, we had been taught a mechanistic view of our physical body when it came to health and disease. I understood there needed to be recognition of the the Light of consciousness housed in the physical body in order to truly understand the healing modalities needed.

As I lay on the couch, all of these thoughts and understandings flowed through my mind, one after another. I realized if we could avail ourselves to various energy healing modalities earlier in our lives, then perhaps we would develop less physical and mental pathology later.

I marveled at all that Jesus had imparted to me about disease. The knowledge felt so familiar. Had I once known this and somehow forgotten it? All that he said had a feeling of innate Truth to it and would serve as a foundation for future growth and greater understandings as I matured spiritually.

Disease had always fascinated me from the time I was a young child. For me, the study of disease had become a doorway into the study of the Infinite. Once I imbibed and understood what I needed to know on disease, Jesus moved to another topic: **Aging.**

Chapter 7

Jesus Speaks

THE SIXTH REVELATION: ON AGING

Then Jesus spoke, **"Now do you understand what aging is all about?"** As he spoke these words, I was given the experience and understanding of aging. I could feel the friction between my mind and body as my mind latched onto thoughts of anger, doubts and fears. As my mind busied itself with one concern or another, I felt how tiring it was. I saw how my emotions took me on a roller coaster ride up and down. I saw how my mind was always thinking so many thoughts at once, even conflicting thoughts of love and hate from one moment to the next. And I was either regretful of the past or worried about the future. I had no idea how to be in the moment. This I realized was the human condition.

The mind always went traveling from one thing to another to try to find happiness. It went from one thought to another, one relationship to another, from one job to another, from one hobby to another, in a dizzying frenetic pace just to have a moment of satisfaction. In the end, it only felt exhausted, disappointed and unfulfilled. I

19

understood how long-held grudges, negative thinking about others and ourselves start in our thoughts and end up as hardened faces and tightened lips.

I further understood these chronic thoughts and feelings took a toll on us mentally and physically, because they interfered with the pure flow of our consciousness, our life-giving energy that fed into the physical body through our chakras. Perhaps if I could quiet my mind, I could live more in the moment of pure being with its rejuvenating power.

I also realized I accepted falling apart as I aged as inevitable. But I wondered, is it inevitable? I knew eventually the body would wear out, but perhaps not as quickly and to such a degree as I had previously thought.

I realized I needed to find a better way to handle the anxieties and thoughts that seemed to have free reign in my mind, so they wouldn't continually turn around and around spewing negativities, wearing me out mentally and physically.

I remembered someone telling me that whenever I felt anxious, I should just start taking deep breaths and then I wouldn't feel so anxious. I wondered how the mind and the breath were related. I thought about tortoises and how they could live to be more than two hundred years old because they only breathe four times a minute. I wondered how we could take that information and apply it to humans to slow down our aging process.

When Jesus finished imparting knowledge about aging, He moved onto another topic: **the Ego.**

Chapter 8

Jesus Speaks

THE SEVENTH REVELATION:
ON THE EGO

Instead of Jesus making a statement about the ego, He went directly into impressing me with His thoughts regarding it, giving me an immediate inner experience and understanding. I saw that there was this thing called ego. I was given to understand the ego as an energetic conceptual construct of identification which we use to identify ourselves as individuals who had personalities with associated likes and dislikes. Upon identifying ourselves in this fashion, we constructed concepts and ideas about the world and what was good and what was bad. We defended what we liked and opposed what we didn't like, all of which we felt a need to voice. We felt a need to voice these opinions because in identifying with the ego as ourselves, we felt our opinions *were* who we were. All of this we did unconsciously. We then felt offended if someone didn't agree with our opinions. Hence there was no end to our suffering!

I became aware for the first time that the ego was something that I had, not something that was an actual part of me. The ego felt separate from the real me. The ego felt like a "tool" I used in order to navigate my way around the world and deal with people. I experienced that it was a reactive tool ready to defend against any real or imagined insult or position contrary to my own ideas. Understanding the ego in this way was a real revelation. Without being conscious of it before, I saw how I used the ego as a way of identifying myself as a woman, a mother, a nurse, a massage therapist. I identified myself as the different roles I played in life and then either congratulated myself for doing a great job or, more often then not, condemned myself for not measuring up. As I lay on the couch, I found myself asking questions: "If I am not the ego, then who is this real me? Is it the role I'm playing at the moment? Could I actually get free of the ego somehow or did I always have to have one?"

I remember being taught from those in the field of psychology that you needed to have an ego or you wouldn't be able to function in the world. Now I questioned if that was true. "Will I always be subject to its whims and fancies, constantly defending its positions and opinions? But how can it be so important to defend my positions and opinions when those change over time? How important can they be? So if I'm not my opinions and ideas and I am not my ego than who am I? My roles? No, those change too."

As I contemplated these questions, the faces of different people I had known appeared in my mind, like on a movie screen. As each person appeared, somehow I could see how they used their egos to define themselves and to defend against their unresolved hurts. I was able to see how their unresolved emotional and mental traumas acted out. For example, I saw how some were hiding their hurt behind anger because the original hurt was unspoken and unresolved. The hurt and anger would then come out sideways in the way they interacted in the world. Some were blatantly disagreeable and hard to get along with. Some were insipidly sweet while rage boiled beneath the surface. Some were controlling. Some used people for their own purposes in very underhanded ways. Some were filled with pride as a compensation due to lack of self-esteem. I saw this was the state of humanity, including myself.

I saw how I had behaved in these different ways at one time or another in my life and I began to sob for my own human predicament and out of remorse for having behaved in these ways in the past. I understood that we humans suffered a great deal protecting our egos. We spent a lot of time trying to get the upper hand, jockeying for positions at the expense of others, arguing and simply making others feel bad while we felt all the better for it. I understood the ego could be a very destructive force.

This experience and understanding of the ego was the beginning of a true spiritual awakening within myself. As I lay on the couch, aware of these thoughts and impressions, I again felt the Presence of an inner love that seemed to be at the core of my being. I felt my hard emotional edges melt away in this love and I felt serene and gentle. Was love the true essence of everything and everyone? It seemed so. But it was so covered over by the antics of the ego.

Now that I had become aware of the predicament I faced with regard to the ego, it dawned on me that I had walked through a portal of understanding into a new awareness and I could never go back to not knowing. I could not justify bad behavior in myself anymore and I could not justify it in others as well. I felt a deeper compassion for myself and everyone in understanding the stronghold the ego had over everyone.

As I lay on the couch, I felt so much Light and love pouring in, around and out of me. I felt totally peaceful and in awe of all that was happening. The deep overwhelming despair I felt earlier had completely left. I felt so relieved. I knew that everything was going to be all right.

Then, the Presence called Jesus left the room just the way it entered, withdrawing His rays through the window and my awareness seemed to return to a normal state of consciousness.

Slowly, I got up and stumbled off the couch feeling completely transformed. I felt like a different person with a different outlook and different understanding of life. Every cell in my body seemed to pulsate with love. I felt so expanded and serene. I decided to get some fresh air. My legs felt wobbly as I headed toward the dining room, through the kitchen and towards the back door to go outside. By now, it was late afternoon. Nothing could have prepared me for what I was about to see as my hand reached for the doorknob and pulled the door open. As I stepped out onto the back porch, I was astonished at what I saw!

Chapter 9

THIS IS PARADISE

I could hardly believe my eyes. As I looked out onto the lawn, I could see a new dimension. Each blade of grass sparkled with Light. Each seemed to be made of shimmering Light particles. I could still see the green blades, but Light sparkled from each one of them! The backyard had a beautiful apple tree in the middle of the lawn and flowerbeds and bushes around the perimeter. I looked at the tree and it sparkled with Light as well, in just the same way as the grass. It was so beautiful, so soft. A squirrel scampered across the lawn and he too radiated with Light! The flowers and everything in my view shimmered with this Light. This Light was filled with a palpable and amazing love. The power of it was so tangible I burst into tears and shouted out loud, "Oh my God, this is Paradise, and we've made it into something else!"

For the first time in my life, I saw the true beauty of this world. I began to sob from this pulsating love that I saw all around. I realized in an instant, that we humans were given the gift of living on this Earth to do something great. We were given this gift of Paradise.

"My God," I thought, "What have we done? We have so polluted the air, water and soil. All of Nature has suffered in our ignorance." I saw how we were given free will and it was our choice to make Earth a paradise or a living hell. It was our choice. Everything had been given to us: The sun, the moon, the stars, the waters, earth, fire, air, wood, flowers, minerals, fruits, vegetables, trees, animals to keep us company and birds to sing us songs. What had we done with it with our relentless ego and ignorance?

I could not believe how blind I had been before. How could I have lived this long and not truly seen the beauty of the world in this way? How could I have not understood the gift of this planet? Having been born into this world, I had taken it for granted.

The sight of all this and my instant understanding had me sobbing all over again. But instead of sobbing in despair, I was sobbing out of a love filled with gratitude. I wanted to apologize to nature, to the animals and flowers and the trees for abusing them with my neglect and ignorance of their innate loving and divine nature. I understood that animals were pure unconditional love. How could they be otherwise?

I stumbled back into the house, overwhelmed with what had been revealed to me. The compassion I felt for humanity and for all nature was unlike anything I had ever experienced before. The power of the love I felt inside shook my body and mind to its very foundation and I had a difficult time containing it. Everywhere I looked, I only saw love, I only felt love, and I only thought love. Every cell in my body continued to vibrate with love. I felt like a huge tuning fork that had been struck with Divine love as it reverberated in my entire being. I felt alive with love. I made my way back into the living room and collapsed onto the couch in a state of loving grace. Instantly, I fell into a deep sleep.

When I awoke, I found a new sense of peace. What had happened to me? What miracle had just occurred? In an effort to get my bearings, I went to the back door and looked out again. This time there was just the green grass, the apple tree and flowers. There was no more shimmering Light. My normal sight returned but my understanding had changed forever. A new day was dawning for me. All the days of the rest of my life would be changed, for I had stepped out of the deep sleep of ignorance onto the path of enlightenment.

This was the day of my spiritual awakening, which would continue to unfold over the years in ways I could never imagine.

Years later, I would hear someone read a poem at a meditation center entitled, The Odes of Solomon (1st or 2nd Century), which truly spoke to my experiences on this day:

The Odes of Solomon (1st or 2nd Century)
*My heart was split, and a flower
appeared; and grace sprang up;
and it bore fruit for my God.
You split me, tore my heart
open, filled me with love.
You poured your spirit into me;
I knew you as I know myself.
Speaking waters touched me
from your fountain, the source of life.
I swallowed them and was drunk
with the water that never dies.
And my drunkenness was insight,
intimacy with your spirit.
And you have made all things new;
you have showed me all things shining.
You have granted me perfect ease;
I have become like Paradise,
a garden whose fruit is joy;
and you are the sun upon me.
My eyes are radiant with your spirit;
my nostrils fill with your fragrance.
My ears delight in your music,
and my face is covered with your dew.*

Blessed are the men and women
who are planted on your earth, in your garden,
who grow as your trees and flowers grow,
who transform their darkness to light.
Their roots plunge into darkness;
their faces turn toward the light.
All those who love you are beautiful;
they overflow with your presence
so that they can do nothing but good.
There is infinite space in your garden;
all men, all women are welcome here;
all they need do is enter.[1]

1"The Odes of Solomon" (p. 24) from THE ENLIGHTENED HEART: AN ANTHOLOGY OF SACRED POETRY, EDITED by STEPHEN MITCHELL. Copyright © 1989 by Stephen Mitchell. Reprinted by permission of HarperCollins Publishers.

Chapter 10

‡ LIFE AFTER AWAKENING: A VEIL REMOVED

In the days that followed, I wondered why I had this visitation from Jesus. Was it just for me or was I to share it? I felt different inside. I felt more love inside, more alive and aware of what was going on around me. Before that, I had felt so separate from people and defensive. Now, I was more relaxed and open. And something else happened that was miraculous. It seemed Jesus removed a "veil of ignorance" from my eyes and I could see and understand things about people. I could see people's troubles when I looked at them. Somehow an inner eye of understanding, compassion and knowing had opened and I could see in people their emotional wounds and corresponding patterns of compensation that had built up over the years. I felt the compensation in the way a person used words and by the look in their eyes. I could literally feel if they were telling the truth or trying to conceal something. If they were trying to conceal something, the energy of the words would feel stuck in my solar plexus. If they were truthful, the energy of the words would flow through me. I could only imagine this is what people meant when they said, "I had a gut feeling."

At first, I was quite shocked that I could see and understand all of this. What before had confused me about other people's behavior had now seemed so obvious and I could easily discern why they acted the way they did. I saw their unresolved suffering so clearly that it was sometimes disturbing to me. I felt privy to feelings that were hidden behind their demeanor. I understood that what I saw of their troubles was just a reflection of the issues they were dealt in life, it was not the real them. The real them was pure Divine love.

My new understandings also required that I continually correct my own thoughts and actions. When I resisted, things would not work so smoothly in my life. I realized much had been given to me and in return much would be expected. I recognized that I would be required to live up to my new understandings; I had to put them into practice on a daily basis.

I marveled at all that had happened. And yet I still had to deal with the mundane world. Bills needed to be paid and my daughter needed to be fed, clothed and loved. Integrating all of this was a challenge. I still struggled with so many issues. For example, I couldn't help but feel like a dismal failure regarding my daughter. I loved her so much and yet the knowledge that I could not give her an intact home life with a mother and a father still haunted me, perhaps because I had so yearned for it for myself.

When I went into work, a few days after Jesus' visitation, I felt so open. I felt so much love for perfect strangers I saw on the street. It was a thrilling feeling unlike anything I had ever experienced. I was like a kid with a new toy. But this was much better, as no one could take it away from me!

People at work noticed that something had happened to me. They said I looked different. They seemed confused and wondered if I had gotten a new haircut or something. I said nothing. A month later, my boss said in an informal conversation among co-workers, "Oh, Mary's discovered love." I was so astounded I didn't say anything. She could see something had happened and even named it love. But it was so much more than that. It was God.

I also had to get used to being inside myself in a whole new way since I could now see and appreciate my own and other people's problems. Before, I spent a lot of time judging others; now I had a whole new feeling of compassion towards others and myself. I became a kinder person. I found myself wishing the best for people who were struggling with life, as I too was struggling. As life presented its challenges day in and day out, the remembrance of the visitation faded more and more into the background.

I never spoke to anyone about my awakening. I felt they would think I was crazy, so I kept it all to myself. Life continued for me, but now I had a larger perspective on it than before and a greater appreciation that there was more to life than met the eye.

I began reading a lot of books on spirituality like *The Tao* and many of Alice Bailey's works like *Esoteric Healing*. I read Shirley MacLaine's *Out on a Limb*. Shirley's book really hit home. I felt out on a limb all right. Unable to express or hold my awakening in some familiar context, I kept what was happening inside a secret. In spite of that, people could tell something was different and they continued to comment about it in rather surprising ways.

I was attending massage school classes which were scheduled on weekends with two week-long retreats each year. This meant that the students got to know each other very well. Very shortly after the awakening, I went on one of the retreats. In one of the sharing groups, a classmate burst into tears and yelled at me saying, "You have so much Light pouring out of you I can hardly stand it!" I was stunned and didn't know what to say. This was all new to me as well. I didn't know how to explain what happened. Others in the group said, "Yeah, you look different. You're more relaxed or something." Another woman in the group, who was usually kind to me, suddenly became very abrupt in our interactions. In a telephone conversation, a few days after I returned home, she explained her behavior. She said, "I could see that something happened to you and I wanted it too. That's why I was so nasty to you." I wish I could have explained to her at the time what had happened, but frankly I didn't have the words for it.

I was quite affected by these reactions, which made me feel more than ever that I did not want to share my experiences. I didn't know how to be anymore. I needed to learn how to integrate all the inner changes. I was also beginning to enjoy solitude a great deal.

It would take a long time for me to adjust to my "new eyes" and new understandings. I told no one, not my family, not friends at school, not my therapist. I was still in therapy trying to sort out my life, but I never once spoke of these experiences; I had never heard anyone else speaking about these kinds of experiences either and I thought I'd be misunderstood.

Life continued with its challenges of day-to-day issues. Things did not really get easier; I just had a better perspective on what was happening. Instead of immediately reacting to whatever someone might say or do, I would reflect more on what was going on and respond more calmly. Of course, this didn't happen every time. I would fall back to my reactive ways more times than not, but I always came back to the Truth of love. I was no longer caught up in the web of ignorance. I now knew that God was at work in all things and all people and my behavior needed to reflect that knowledge.

Sometimes I would feel life was more difficult being awake because now I could not blame other people for how my life was going. At other times, I was so grateful for being awakened from the suffering that came from thinking, "I'm a failure, life has no meaning and God is dead!" Also, knowing the deep love that existed in everyone and in everything brought me comfort and hope.

In the meantime, I was still exploring alternative therapies. Since Reiki energy treatments seemed to help me so much, I decided to take a Reiki workshop and incorporate this form of healing into my massage treatments. A few days after completing the Reiki course, I had another remarkable experience.

Chapter 11

THE MIRACLE OF THE BIRDS

I was out one afternoon riding my bicycle and stopped alongside the road to briefly watch some kids playing softball. As I was standing over my bike with one foot on the pavement for balance and the other still on a pedal, for some reason I looked down at my foot that was on the ground. There within inches of my foot, was a wounded sparrow. Only one of his wings seemed to be working and he was going around in circles trying to get off the ground. Without thinking, I swooped him up in my hand and held him next to my heart, hoping the sound of my heartbeat might calm him. Off I went on my bike heading home. I really wasn't sure what I was going to be able to do for him, but I couldn't leave him on the ground to die.

I parked my bike and went into the house. I found a box, emptied it out and placed the bird inside. He didn't attempt to move very much; I'm sure partly out of fright and partly because of his wounds. As I looked closer, I could see that he had lost the sight in one of his eyes. I thought for sure this bird was going to die. What was I going to do? I put some water in a small bowl and got some grass from outside to line the box. Then I called a friend of mine who had sent me to the Reiki classes. "Oh," she laughed, "Birds especially get attracted to people who open up to the Reiki energy." She knew I just finished taking my Reiki class. "Give it some Rescue Remedy and hold it in your hands and give it Reiki." After hanging up the phone, I didn't know what to think. Really, I thought my friend was a little goofy. But what did I have to lose?

I did Reiki on the bird as instructed and fed it some of the remedy. Later, I went to the store to get some birdseed. I never expected that sparrow to live, but I did Reiki on it a few times a day over the next two days. Every time I came home from work, I rushed to the box, sure I would find the sparrow dead.

On the third day, I came home as usual and went to the box. It was empty! "Oh no," I thought, "The bird got out of the box and is dead somewhere in a corner." I went searching for the bird and lo and behold, it was perched in the livingroom on a chair! I could not believe my eyes. It started flying around the room. How could that be? It had been so injured. It was a miracle. I was totally astounded and amazed.

Now that it had recovered, the next task was to release it outside. But how? First I had to catch it. And how would I do that? I brought his box into the livingroom, where he was still perched on a chair. I decided to try to talk to the bird while wondering if that would really work. "Look," I said out loud, "You've got to fly over here onto this box. If you do and you let me catch you, I'll release you outside. Don't worry, I won't hurt you."

To my utter and complete astonishment, the bird flew over and perched on the box! With one calm, swift motion, I gently picked him up in my hand and walked to the back door. I looked at him and saw that he still had only one eye to see with, but at least the wound of the injured eye had closed over. I walked down the stairs off the back porch and stood under the apple tree and released him.

What a sight! I opened my hands and watched him fly to

one of the lower branches of the apple tree. He flew so strongly. I could feel myself choking on a sob and finally just let myself cry. I wished him well and felt such a powerful love between us. He perched for a while on the branch and looked at me, as if to say a final goodbye, then swiftly flew away to another tree next door. His wing had healed completely and even though he had only one eye for sight, he seemed to navigate just fine.

In that moment, I felt the bird and I had communicated our love and appreciation of each other using telepathy. When I went inside, I looked up the word telepathy in a dictionary. It was defined as, "the supposed sending of messages from one mind to another by some means other than by speaking or seeing."

My experience with birds was not over yet. The very next morning, just as I was about to open the door to the back porch to leave for work, there was a pigeon standing right in front of it, waiting to get into my house! I thought, "My God, what does he want? Did he get a referral from the sparrow? Could my friend have been right about birds sensing this healing energy?" I shooed him away a little, so he wouldn't come into my kitchen. He moved away to the other side of the porch but wouldn't leave. I realized he was ill.

I wasn't sure what to do, so I decided to go back into the house and called animal control. They seemed rather perplexed when I tried to explain how the bird wanted to come into my house because he was ill, but they promised to come over and take care of the situation. In the meantime, I had to go off to work. I don't know what ever happened to the pigeon but I stopped doubting my friend and what she had to say after that.

My experiences with sparrows would continue. A few years later, when I was at a meditation retreat, I had another astounding experience. In the early morning, I was walking out onto an open-aired porch with some friends. There were tables and chairs scattered around where people ate breakfast. I noticed a few sparrows sitting on tabletops eating the last of some crumbs. My friends walked ahead of me to find a table. The sparrows immediately flew away, all except one. Everyone else was on the other end of the porch, but I was lagging behind because I noticed the sparrow. He sat on top of the table and we just looked at one another with great interest.

As we stared at each other, everything seemed to go into slow motion. I knew I could put my finger out and he would sit on it. Slowly, I lowered my right hand to the sparrow's feet with my finger acting as a perch. He hopped on effortlessly! With the sparrow safely sitting on my finger, I brought him up to my eye level. We stared at each other very intently. I was in awe; I think he was in awe as well. The world seemed to stand still. I almost felt like he was going to "talk" to me.

Just at that moment one of my friends noticed this and walked over while stretching her hand out saying she also wanted to hold the bird. As she did, the bird flew away. Then time returned to normal speed and my friend apologized for interrupting. She looked at me rather strangely as if to say, "What the heck are you doing?" No one else in the group had noticed what happened.

As I mentioned, before he flew away, I felt the sparrow was about to communicate something telepathically. Perhaps he could sense I wouldn't hurt him. Perhaps he knew of the incident that had happened with the other sparrow a few years back. I remembered hearing once that every action we performed and every word we spoke was recorded in our consciousness. Did the sparrow sense that? I don't know, but I found the whole experience profoundly moving.

At yet another time, I was sitting meditating in a lobby during a lunch break at work. I heard the sound of a sparrow. I opened my eyes and noticed there was a sparrow sitting on a limb of an indoor ficus tree. I knew if he didn't somehow get outside, he would die. As I approached him, I told him I wouldn't hurt him and if he would just be still, I would carry him outside. To my astonishment, he let me do just that! I took him in my hands and placed him near my heart and brought him outside to some nearby hedges, where he quickly took flight. A man had noticed this and just looked at me with an amazed smile on his face. I smiled back and went inside to finish my meditation while contemplating what had just happened. By now I felt I had a way with birds.

It seemed this deeper connection with birds and nature was a direct result of my spiritual awakening. I no longer held the concept of a separateness between nature and me. I could feel on a cellular level that I was in nature and nature was in me. I felt we belonged to a continuum of life rather than as separate unrelated components. I realized that anything done to nature would also have an impact on me and visa versa.

Chapter 12

EINSTEIN'S THEORY OF RELATIVITY:
$E=MC^2$

It was May 1985 and I continued imbibing my revelatory visit from Jesus. I was still processing being awakened to a whole new energy system in my body and to a whole new way of seeing, thinking and feeling. My inner emotional walls of defensiveness continued to crumble day by day. These walls had been built to survive my childhood and the years that followed. It was now time for the walls to come down, because instead of protecting me, I had become their prisoner.

During this time, I graduated from massage school. I had hoped to go on and learn more at the school as an apprentice teacher, but there were many feelings of discontent between my class and the school. I, as well as others in my class, were not invited to return. In the past, I would have been completely devastated by something like that. It's not that my feelings weren't hurt, because I felt deeply hurt, but I could be more accepting of the situation. I had also learned by now that when one's karma was over with a group or a person, it was over. It was analogous to letting the air out of a balloon — there was just no more energy left in it. Still, I cried almost every day as a way to release tears that needed to be shed. As time passed, life presented new opportunities. I realized I would not have been open to them if I had stayed at the school.

I spent a great deal of time by myself in nature, sitting outside in silence. This silence allowed me to experience nature more acutely. There was a state park in Rockport, Massachusetts that had a beach filled with huge boulders which seemed to have been there from the beginning of time. Still cleansing emotionally, I went there for comfort. As I sat on one of the rocks, I began to feel its innate nature —solid, reliable, constant and even wise. I realized these rocks had been there for thousands of years and had been silent witnesses to all the comings and goings of the ages. Many people had sat on these rocks with all their troubles and life stories just like me. Yet these rocks remained neither disturbed nor elated, they just sat in their peaceful state, nothing shook them. They did not go up and down in their state like I did. I thought my state should be more like a rock—solid, stable and content, during the inevitable ups and downs of life. I could almost hear the rock speak its wisdom. I remembered my experience of the light particles when I looked out onto the backyard. I realized these rocks were also made of light particles filled with an innate wisdom that could be conveyed.

As I mentioned before, one of the most remarkable effects after Jesus' revelations was that my eyes were cleansed to see things that were troubling people. I began to yearn to see a clear pair of eyes, but was unable to find them in anyone.

I really wanted to understand what had happened to me with the Light. I wanted to better understand my own experience with Jesus. I was less identified with having only a physical body. Now I knew I also had a Light body. The closest intellectual concept I could equate with my experience of the Light and my physical body, was Einstein's theory of relativity: $E=mc^2$, energy equals mass times the speed of light. I felt this equation somehow related to my experience of having a physical body *and* a Light body at the same time. But how? How did this matter I called my physical body relate to the Light and to God and science? I wanted a scientific explanation to comprehend in my mind what I knew to be true in my heart, that love and Light were all.

I was wishing I could find someone who could explain all of this to me. I wanted to understand what it was I so longed to see in a pair of eyes—perhaps it was clarity. I also began to use a phrase called "Energy Medicine" to describe my own healing process. Working with the energy in the body through massage, Reiki and acupuncture was a field of medicine I felt could truly help people heal. But in 1985, not many understood this as deeply as I had experienced it.

Life continued to change and I was downsized out of my job during an administrative reorganization, but was happy to leave because I really didn't like being there. I received a little severance pay to keep me going and my practice as a massage therapist began to grow.

I happened to see an advertisement for a free lecture on Energy Medicine. This concept of Energy Medicine had been on my mind for a while now. The ad said there would be a panel of practitioners who would talk about the energy in the body: an acupuncturist, a chiropractor, a medical doctor, who had studied in China to see how acupuncture worked, and an energy bodyworker. I attended the lecture to see if what they had to say might give me a better understanding of my spiritual experiences. All the lecturers were interesting, but for me, one stood out. What next occurred riveted my attention and changed my life in a way I could not have imagined.

As each person at the presentation stood to speak, they stated their name and introduced themselves, all except one. This one healer, the energy bodyworker, stood up and said, "$E=mc^2$, Einstein's Theory of Relativity. Einstein proved that matter, energy and the speed of light are related." He went on to explain how the physical body was made of matter and that the body was energy as a dense temporary expression. He said that the light energy which gave the body life was matter in its most refined expression. He further said that everything was made of energy and that light, energy and matter were inextricably linked. He explained that essentially matter was only a transformation of light energy.

I couldn't believe it! Here was the answer to my question about Einstein's theory and its relation to my experiences. A sense of urgency took over my entire being. I had to make an appointment to see him. I ran up to him as soon as there was a break. I remember grabbing his arm and saying "I must see you." I made an appointment to meet with him for a healing session a few days later.

Another turning point in my life was about to occur. Something extraordinary and transforming was about to happen. On the day of the appointment with the healer I would also meet someone else who would change my life, yet again. This meeting was pre-ordained. I was about to meet my destiny. This meeting would clearly be a continuation of my visitation with Jesus two years prior. Through this person, I would come to understand so much more of what Jesus had imparted. Grace was about to enter my life again very powerfully and change me forever.

Chapter 13

IT'S GOD AGAIN

I counted the days until the healing session, intensely curious as to what might happen. Finally the day came. As I walked into the healer's office, we spoke polite hellos and he excused himself for a minute to speak with someone in the other room. While he was gone, immediately I was drawn to a picture hanging on the wall. To say I was riveted was an understatement. I felt drawn to that picture like a magnet.

It was a picture of a women's face and as I looked into her seemingly endless eyes, I heard myself saying out loud, "I know her and she knows me." I had a flash in my mind of a lifetime I had spent as a monk with this person and I knew it had been a very happy lifetime. As I searched her eyes in the picture, I realized that these were the eyes I had been looking for! They were clear eyes, open eyes, eyes that seemed to go on forever, eyes that knew everything about energy and Truth. Yes, I had found the eyes! But who was this? And what did this mean? Was she alive? I hoped she was.

Just then the healer walked into the room and I was still

staring at the picture. I said to him, "I know her and she knows me. Who is that anyway? Is she alive? She knows everything there is to know about energy and Truth." He answered, "That could be. Yes, she's alive. Do you want to meet her? She'll be in Boston in two weeks." "Yeah, I want to meet her. Is she a monk?" He said, yes, and that he'd be in touch when she arrived.

I was thrilled at the possibility of meeting her. I wondered in my mind if this meant we were to continue the spiritual teachings from the time I had been her monk in that past life. I secretly hoped it would be true.

At the same time, I noticed a little dog had followed the healer into the room. I was immediately captivated by him, because he looked like the dog I had as a child, a dog that I had to put to sleep after sixteen years as my best friend. Upon sight of him, I started crying. Then I started sobbing uncontrollably. I was shocked to realize that I was still holding the almost unbearably painful memory of losing my dog, of holding her in my arms as the vet put her to sleep with an injection. It was more than I could bear. Since I was nineteen, these feelings had been buried very deep in a place that seemed inaccessible up until this point. As it happened, that was the same time in my life when I found out I was pregnant and had to leave the country to arrange for an adoption.

I told the healer about the memory of my dog and my pregnancy and he started immediately working with my energy. At first he just held me as I sobbed and told me to breathe deeply and follow my breath. As I did that, he made swooshing sounds with his breath that seemed to clear and help move my emotions. I remembered that emotions were energy and energy could be worked with by transforming and transmuting it. Perhaps that's what he was doing with his breath.

He then had me lie down on a massage table on my back and asked me to follow my breath and stay with the emotions. At my request, he had his little dog come up on the table to lie next to me. This was the beginning of the longest healing session I ever had. It lasted six hours. I felt as if I was clearing out every deep hurt I had ever felt in this lifetime and in others. Layer after layer came up. Would this ever end? I knew I wasn't just crying about the painful events in my life to rehash them, but to release them, to cleanse them from the depths of my soul.

I sobbed and sobbed. To my surprise at certain times he sobbed too. He seemed to be helping me experience the feelings out. At one point, a few hours into the treatment, he said, "I can feel your daughter, the one you gave up for adoption, in your energy field. I'm not supposed to tell you. Usually I don't. But I feel drawn to tell you. You have a very strong spiritual connection with her. She wants me to tell you something. She wants me to tell you she doesn't hate you for giving her up. She understands and she loves you." I felt my heart break into thousands of pieces as he said those words. I continued to sob and he did too. Both of us seemed involved in this healing. A few more hours passed like this.

Finally, it neared the end of the session and I felt calm and purified from releasing so much. The healer stood at my feet. His abdomen touched the soles of my feet and he instructed me to breathe slowly.

All of a sudden I felt a Divine Presence. There was a flood of Light pouring into the top of my head, flowing down through my arms and entire body, through my legs and out my feet. I thought, "It's God again! But why is He here?" It felt like the time Jesus had visited me, only stronger. When I felt this Light pour out my hands and feet, I wondered if the healer felt it too, but I said nothing. I thought of the image of Jesus with Light coming from his hands and feet. "Oh, I thought, so that's how Jesus healed. He healed using this Light." I thought of the halos around the heads of saints and realized that it was this same Light. I felt so peaceful and content. I wanted it to last forever. I envisioned a picture of the Blessed Mother Mary and remembered seeing Light coming from her hands and feet too. She had the same Divine Light as Jesus.

The Light scintillated inside every cell of my body and ran along every pathway parallel to my nervous system. I realized all of these pathways of Light corresponded with the meridians I had seen on acupuncture charts. "My God," I thought, "The meridians do exist as Light, the Chinese were right!" I felt so much love inside me, so much Light. I felt extremely happy and very comforted. After a few minutes the experience subsided and the healer left the room so that I could rest before getting up.

By the time he returned, I was off the table and sitting on the floor. I felt like a rag doll from all the crying but also very light and quite peaceful. As he sat down next to me he said, "Hail Mary, full of Grace." I was astounded and wondered why he had said that. But I didn't want to ask because I felt so protective of my experience with the Light and I did not want to get into a conversation about it. I wondered if he really could feel what I felt. Then he said, "You have a lot of Grace coming your way." I thought, "I do? I wonder why he said that." Still, I said nothing. I felt so wonderful after the session. I went home and slept more deeply than I had in months.

Chapter 14

MEETING THE MONK

As promised, the healer called me to meet the woman monk that I saw in the picture, when she arrived in Boston. When I met her, I felt she was indeed my spiritual teacher, although I had no conscious thought of needing one before seeing her picture; I simply wanted to find a pair of eyes, or so I thought. She happened to give a talk on the ego the day I met her. I listened with great interest and found that what Jesus had said to me two years prior was exactly what she was saying now.

Finally, I found someone who could completely understand the revelations I had had with Jesus. It was an enormous relief to me, for I felt I could tell her anything and she would completely understand. I knew she was my teacher in a past life and we had come together again so I could complete something. I didn't know what that was, but I did know for certain, that the peace and love I felt in her Presence was something I wanted for myself.

Another strange thing happened in the days that followed. For hours on end, I started spontaneously writing spiritual poetry. I never had to labor to find the right words, they just seemed to pour into me and through the pen onto the paper. When this happened, I always felt so peaceful and happy. Writing poetry was a way for me to express the spiritual experiences I had been given. Writing acted as an outlet.

The following poems arose from those earliest experiences. The first poem speaks to how I felt the day of Jesus' revelations. The second poem speaks to the experience of my chakras opening and what I saw when I opened the door to my backyard. The third poem explains how I changed and could view things differently as I went about my daily life. The last two poems express my reaction to having finally found the pair of eyes in the picture of the monk.

Slumber
My Lord shook me
From limb to limb
to awaken me.
Drifting in and out
of coma
My Lord never left
my side.
Awaken!
How long can you slumber?

Pure Delight
Chakra one
Chakra two
Chakra three and four.
Up the ladder,
Down the ladder,
Can you tell me more?
Chakra five, six and seven,
when your Consciousness is Pure,
you will find that Earth's a Heaven
waiting at your door.

Twin Passions
Dispassion and Compassion,
Twin passions
For you see
You need them both
to view
the world
With perfect
clarity.

The Teacher's Eyes
Endless vision
Piercing my limitations
Cajoling the Soul
To release its bounty.

Eyes of Fire
Soul's Alchemist,
Burning, blazing
into Gold,
Purifying
all that's old.

After meeting my teacher, I learned how to meditate and chant God's name. I began reading spiritual scriptures like *Patanjali's Yoga Sutras, Shankara's Crest-Jewel of Discrimination* and the *Bhagavad Gita,* that although written hundreds of years ago, were just as relevant for me in understanding my true nature. I learned how to worship myself with the knowledge that God lived inside me as me. I felt as if a breath of fresh air had entered my life and I was about to begin life anew. I felt as if I were on the brink of a new and exciting adventure. It was now June of 1986.

Chapter 15

THE PREPARATION

Over the summer I completely immersed myself in the spiritual practices of meditation, contemplation, chanting and offering service at the meditation center where I had met my teacher. All of these practices felt very familiar and very natural. It felt so wonderful to meditate. I was given a spiritual initiation from my teacher, which made meditation alot easier; I could sit down and let my mind rest for a change. Meditation helped me enormously in my life. I felt more focused, balanced and grounded, and I was certain meditation aided in helping me to land a great job at MIT that fall. I loved my new boss; he looked a lot like the Dalai Lama and had a pleasant demeanor. Finally I found a job and a boss that I truly enjoyed.

Meditation became something I did during my lunch break at work. In the warm weather, I would sit outside in a quiet courtyard. I particularly enjoyed basking in the sunlight amongst the foliage while feeding the many sparrows that gathered for my leftovers. Their little faces melted any tension I felt from the morning's work; they were so adorable and full of innocence. Sparrows perched on the branches of a nearby apple tree that was actually a descendant of the tree that Newton had sat under when an apple fell on his head, inspiring him to understand the laws of gravity. Surrounding myself with beauty and inspiration in this way, my mind quickly settled down into my lunchtime meditation.

During one of these lunchtime meditations, I had a breakthrough in my meditation practice. Before the breakthrough, during my meditations a black wall of fear would arise from within. I would mentally pull back from it and then stop my meditation. I would begin again, and again it would happen. After six months of this, something finally changed. I was finally able to break through this fear. On that day, the black wall of fear appeared as always, but instead of moving away from it, I finally had the courage to move towards it. As I did, the wall of fear disappeared like fog and I emerged into a shining Light. I could hardly believe it! The Light was so bright and I felt immediately peaceful. Never again would I encounter that wall of fear. My self-effort was rewarded with a greater sense of inner peace in my meditations and throughout my daily activities.

I also offered service in the form of cooking, cleaning and administrative skills at the meditation center. I noticed that no matter what service I offered, I always felt remarkably happy afterwards. How could cleaning toilets make someone feel so joyful? The mystery of service as a spiritual practice always amazed me. My mind would feel transformed from negative thoughts to positive ones as I performed the most mundane tasks. Any gloom from the day would disappear; it simply melted away without me even thinking about it.

Chanting was something familiar to me as I had sung in choirs in my youth and adult years, and so it immediately felt like a familiar practice. In the past, singing always put me in a good mood, but chanting seemed to have a more powerful energy. Chanting combined music and singing with sacred mantras that vibrated at the highest level of consciousness. As I chanted, cares would melt from my mind and heart. During the chant and afterwards, I noticed I would gain a clearer perspective on whatever problems I was experiencing in my life. For example, I would get answers to questions, like how to handle a client at work or how to rework an organizational problem. Nothing seemed too mundane. I also experienced that chanting gave my mind greater focus and I accomplished more at work in a shorter time.

When I first began these spiritual practices, I felt as if I was living two lives: a worldly life and a spiritual life. But the more I did the practices, in the next few years, I realized there was only one life and that all life was sacred and spiritual. I realized that washing dishes for my family was just as spiritual as praying. It was all in one's attitude. I became aware of my actions as an expression of love; it was a little shift but it made a world of difference in how I felt inside.

I realized everything in my life could be an offering and little things counted the most: a kind word to a stranger, holding a door open for the next person, letting someone go ahead of me in line at the grocery store when they had only one item. I realized that God lived in the details of life and it was how I lived the details that seemed to make all the difference. I noticed I was becoming a kinder and kinder person slowly but surely.

Still, life was not without its challenges, as I continued to grow emotionally and spiritually. My ego was quite strong in the form of self-judgment, pride and a critical approach to things. I also tended to be an impatient person. I began to understand the impatience came more from an underlying anxiety that played out in rushing around to get as much done as possible in the shortest amount of time. I realized at some point I could still get things done in an efficient manner without rushing. In order to change the habit of rushing, I needed to look at the underlying anxiety that was at the root of it. The pride, negativity and impatience needed to be confronted. I needed to face down all these impostors and find the real me, the loving me.

Part of facing these impostors was having the willingness to look at myself honestly and say "Yes, I *am* like that aren't I." When I did that, any resistance to change would melt away along with the mental habits. I realized these negative mental habits were not the real me anyway, so there was no need to hold on to them. It seemed these companions of the ego could not live in the face of scrutiny and self-inquiry. Even though this process was very challenging, at the end of a growth spurt, I would feel so much better—as if I had unburdened many lifetimes of suffering. It seemed I had become a student of meditation, chanting, service and self-inquiry and I loved it!

Little did I know at this time, all this inner and outer immersion in the spiritual practices was a preparation for what was to come. Little did I know I was about to experience the most awesome event of my life. This experience would change me yet again in the most profound ways. This event would foretell what awaited all humanity. What happened to me was so extraordinary that I never could have imagined it.

Chapter 16

SELF-REALIZATION

Two years passed filled with dedication and devotion to the spiritual practices. It was the summer of 1988 and I decided to take some time away from home to attend a spiritual retreat. I yearned to be with my teacher, who had just returned after being away for two years. I very much enjoyed studying and contemplating the teachings of the spiritual masters and I signed up for a course at the retreat site. It was a beautiful day in July. I was sitting outside by myself on the retreat grounds during a lunch break. In my mind, I was repeating some words that were given by my teacher during the course, as a way to clear out old negative mental habits. At the same time, I was reading from a book about the Soul and the personality. In the book, entitled *"The Light of the Soul, The Yoga Sutras of Patanjali"*, by Alice A. Bailey, it said that the ego-personality must be replaced by the Soul as the driver of the physical vehicle, the body. I wondered what it would be like not to be driven by my ego-personality. I wondered what it might be like to simply let my ego-personality melt into my Soul and let my Soul lead the way. I found it a totally fascinating concept and was utterly captivated by it. My thoughts totally immersed in contemplation, I had full faith that this could happen and that I would like it to happen to me.

Just then, as I sat quietly under the shade of a huge pine tree, the most wondrous thing happened! What I am about to say is simply astonishing and at the same time it seemed like the most natural thing in the world. What I am about to recount is the ultimate experience in any human life. This experience would give me the understanding as to why I kept coming back to this Earth, lifetime after lifetime.

Fully engrossed in the book and deep in contemplation, suddenly I felt a Presence come over me. It hovered over my head and began to shower me with a golden Light that felt like the sweetest nectar I have ever experienced. This golden Light slowly showered downward over my head and shoulders. I knew in a flash this was God!

So many things began to happen all at once as God spoke these exact words: ***"Here is your Divinity, the Divinity that awaits all Mankind. Your Soul wants full expression now. This is the Presence. This is the Living Presence. This is Living. This is real."***

It was a voice like I had never heard before. It was male sounding and yet it seemed beyond any quality of maleness in humans I had known. This pure God voice was very soft, divinely healing and completely consoling. This Presence poured over me like liquid Light, like golden nectar and immediately I became deeply peaceful.

As God spoke each sentence, different experiences and understandings automatically awakened inside me, the very same way it had with Jesus, only this time more powerfully. As God spoke "Here is your Divinity, the Divinity that awaits all Mankind", my heart leapt with joy that Divinity could and did indeed belong to all of Humanity! I remembered Jesus' teaching that, "The Kingdom of God is within", but I had no idea *this* was what He meant!

The degree of Divinity was awesome to experience. The sheer Divine power was unbelievable! I thought, "This lives inside every human being? How amazing. How astounding! So much Divine power! How could this be?" But it was true. I knew beyond any shadow of doubt it was true. And when God said, "the Divinity that awaits all Mankind" it was clear that it was Mankind's destiny to reclaim this Divinity. I likened our hidden Divinity to having a blanket covering a piece of furniture. The furniture was still there, but you couldn't see it, because the blanket was over it. But if you peeled back the blanket, there was the furniture. I understood in the same way, our ego-personality-mind was covering our Divinity like a blanket.

I knew beyond any shadow of a doubt and with firm conviction that we were here to reclaim our Divinity. I knew I had come back to this Earth to rediscover it as a permanent state of consciousness, a permanent state of awareness. For so long, for so many lifetimes I had become used to having an ego-personality-mind as my identity, convinced in every lifetime that the particular person and role I played was the real me. I had always lived thinking I was a particular person, nothing more, nothing less. How could it have been otherwise? I didn't know any other way. I didn't know anything else was possible. But now, I knew what was possible and still I could hardly believe such a thing was true! But here I was living the indisputable Truth, the greatest Truth of human existence: Divinity.

I had no idea, truly no concept of this enormous omniscience living within a human body. To say it was astounding is an understatement. Truly words cannot contain or express what was revealed to me. I kept thinking, "Oh my God, so this is what Jesus, the Saints, Buddha, Ramakrishna, Confucius and all the Great Ones were talking about. Oh my God, Oh my God!" I was amazed and totally astonished. I felt elated, unbelievably happy and buoyantly joyous! The power, bliss and ecstasy that surged through every cell in my being made me feel very, very happy, enormously joyful and completely whole. I was filled with the wisdom of the Ancient Ones. I *was* the wisdom of the Ancient Ones. So was all of humanity. I realized it was our time to lay claim to our Divine inheritance and knowledge of the Truth within.

When God stated, "This is the Presence, This is the Living Presence", I felt the Light energy filter down from my head all the way down my body inside and out. When it reached the bottom of my spine, all the energy started traveling back up my spine to my head. I had heard of the Kundalini, the spiritual energy that rested at the lowest chakra at the end of the spine, but now I was experiencing it in all its fullness! As it started moving up my spine, it felt like a carpet of energy rolling up, taking with it all my fears, all my physical sexual desire, all my psychological needs for others to support me, all my feelings of separation, all my concerns and all the issues of my life as this individual person. All the issues that concerned my ego-personality-mind as Mary were being rolled up in that energy. The script of life as Mary was being rolled up.

This energy took up everything in its wake until it finally reached the space between my eyebrows. There, something seemed to open with Divine permission and the Kundalini energy went further to the very top of my head. All of a sudden I had the thought, the experience and the complete, total understanding, "I am God, I am God!" I no longer felt, I am Mary with such and such a life. Now I knew beyond any doubt I WAS GOD! With that, a flood of nectarean golden Light flowed like a continuous waterfall from the Heavens downward into the energy center (chakra) located at top of my head, which opened to greet it. I had remembered that Spiritual Masters were sometimes referred to as the "Fountainhead". I was now experiencing the source of this Fountainhead: God.

The waterfall of Light gushed downward flowing from my head chakra forcing my heart center open. All of a sudden, my heart chakra burst open. The Light poured out of my heart like water gushing from a huge fire hose. Immediately, I felt my entire energy field spreading out, expanding in all directions about 100 yards. The Light felt like an ocean of pure compassion endlessly pouring out like the Sun. This compassion poured out of my heart in an unceasing flow. I knew in that instant I had become God! In that instant recognition of my Godness, I experienced a state of unity consciousness. I was aware that the awareness of being God was the only True existence. I was aware that all things came from God. In this state, I felt completely one with God, without any feeling of separateness from God. There was no me and God, there was only God. Now there was only One. My single identity as Mary had been absorbed into my true essence: God.

To have the experience was also to be given the Divine knowledge that went with this state. This unity consciousness felt like my natural state, the true home of my awareness. It simply was me. I understood that being Mary was a role I took on that fit the ego-personality-mind, while the essence of who I was was Divine Consciousness. It felt natural and normal to be in a Divine state of contentment, bliss, perfection and unity. It felt more natural than being in the state of the fearful ego-driven personality-mind. The ego-personality-mind state felt like a terrible suffering, a personal hell. Divinity felt like home and I was elated to finally be back home, existing here in this physical body as God. This was the Truth of who I was. This was the Truth of all humanity. This was the Truth beyond religion. This was what was before religion came into being.

I knew beyond any doubt, that if anyone had come near me at this moment and touched me, they too would have felt the power of this enormous Divine energy. They would have simply been ignited by it! In other words, they would have experienced it in their own conscious awareness that they themselves were Divine.

I swayed inwardly with a feeling of bliss—the pure ecstasy of knowing I AM. I AM. I AM That I AM. What joy, what peace, what contentment! I felt totally fulfilled. I felt totally pure, beyond any need of outward support and therefore, beyond any motive. I understood this was what the great spiritual masters had discovered for themselves: the Truth of their being—God, Brahman. I realized this was what we as humanity were to here to discover, as this was what we already were. I knew most of us weren't aware of this in our conscious every day waking state. I knew most of us were only aware of being a particular person. I understood that humanity was stuck in the dream of the ego-personality and we needed to wake up to our true Self, our true nature. I realized the time and opportunity to do so was at hand. This state was our True inheritance that we needed to lay claim to.

While I was in this state of ecstasy and Godness, I looked down at my body and saw a glow of golden Light coming from my bare arms and hands surrounding all my flesh. I marveled that I could see this. I knew this Light was my True body. The flesh in and of itself looked dead. The Light surrounding my physical body was what was alive. The flesh was a temporary physical temple to house this Light. It was the Light that animated the body and gave it life. All of this was astounding. Yet feeling and seeing all this seemed so natural. It felt like a remembering. This Light energy was indeed "The Living Presence" and being in this state was indeed "Living" and this Light of Divinity was indeed "real" as God had spoken.

I remembered again this Light was what was portrayed as the halo often seen in pictures of Saints surrounding their heads and coming from their hands and feet. I realized that we too were Saints and the Light inside our physical temples was all the same Divine Light! Yes it was true!

I felt alive in a way I had never experienced before. I felt truly alive in my being as God. Instead of feeling myself as my physical body and my problems, I experienced myself as the Light. I was truly alive as Light. I felt free from all concerns. I felt I had come home. I felt completely free from fear. I never realized how much fear I carried around until I was in this Divine state and free of it. In fear's place, there was profound Divine, pure, motiveless love and compassion.

I realized I had crossed over from mere human consciousness belonging to the human kingdom, to Divine consciousness belonging to the Divine kingdom, from where all humanity had originated. We were all Saints in essence, being readied to wake up. It didn't matter what religion one belonged to; this was something that was there before religion and would be there after religion. Yes, that was my experience. This indeed was the great destiny of humanity, the great destiny waiting to be discovered inside each person. I knew this beyond any doubt.

In comparison, the human state of consciousness I had known for so many years and lifetimes felt like being in exile, like living in a strange world, mixed with so many emotions, desires, distresses and conflicts. It felt like a terrible suffering. I did not feel at home there. Instead, now I realized I had found my true home inside my very own awareness! I had indeed finally come home and now I felt totally at home as God.

I realized in this moment that I was beyond suffering. I realized that all suffering came from being out of union with one's innate Divine essence: God. I knew human consciousness consisted of doubt, fear, pride, jealousy, motive, need, possessive love, lack, feeling imperfect and separate. Surely I had suffered those. I knew even human kindness and love could be tinged with motive. I reflected how human consciousness encompassed blame, hatred, distinctions like right and wrong, good and bad and was driven by the ego-personality.

I understood we must use our human lives to once again return to our Divine state while still living in our physical bodies. I knew beyond any doubt that that was the whole point of our existence—to rediscover and return to our true Self while in the midst of living our lives. We were not meant to go to a mountaintop, we were meant to go inside our consciousness to re-discover and lay claim to the essence and source of that consciousness—Divinity, God. Then, all sense of suffering would disappear.

My experience of Divine consciousness consisted of pure fearlessness, total fulfillment, and a feeling of wholeness without need of support. It was beyond the pairs of opposites, such as good and bad. It consisted of the blissful knowledge that we were God. It encompassed a Divine compassion that ego-driven human consciousness could not know or imagine for it did not live in ego-driven consciousness.

I likened this awakening of Divine consciousness to finding the pot of gold at the end of the rainbow. We needed to find the pot of gold at the end of the rainbow inside us. I realized what lay behind the symbolism of finding a pot of gold at the end of a rainbow was the knowledge that the seven main chakras located along our spinal column had a color associated with each of them. I knew these colors comprised the seven colors of the rainbow. I realized we were literally walking rainbows. The pot of gold at the end of the rainbow was the pot of Divine Light located in the head region, the crown chakra. This crown chakra was where our Divinity rested waiting to be accessed, waiting to be rediscovered and reclaimed by us. It was already present within us. It was present within our human body in the form of Light.

As my experience of Divinity continued, I experienced the wisdom and understandings contained in the Light. I was *impressed* with the understanding of the kingdoms: mineral, vegetable, animal, human and Divine. I understood that as humans, it was our divine duty to rise up and reclaim our Divine kingdom through Self-Realization. We needed to realize that we were the great Self, God, the One living in time, but beyond time; the One living in this world, but not of this world. When humans experienced Self-Realization, the other kingdoms would evolve as well. I knew only the human kingdom was capable of Self-Realization. The mineral, vegetable and animal kingdoms did not have this ability. Therefore, all the other kingdoms depended on us to evolve spiritually. I understood we were the caretakers of this earth. It was our responsibility to wake up and reclaim our true home, the Divine kingdom within. All things would become like new in the presence of awakened Divinity.

As my experience of Divinity continued, I noticed more fully that physical desire left me. I did not realize how I carried, on a subtle and not so subtle level, the physical desire for contact with another human body. It seemed like this desire had a life of its own. It seemed as if it were a feeling constantly playing like background music. I realized that in human relations, intercourse was as close to any kind of an instant feeling of a bliss-like state that one could have. But it was in no way like this Divine state. One could not imagine while enjoying the physical pleasures as a human, that there was something far superior to them. I could not have imagined this myself. But here I was in a state of total bliss without a trace of physical desire. It felt like such a relief. I felt unimaginably happy and fulfilled.

I thought about how the culmination of physical desire in orgasm was a fleeting moment of physical satisfaction which faded quickly, leaving one wanting more in an endless cycle of desire and need. Unless one could imagine that there was a way out of this unending desire, into a permanent state of bliss, one would not seek to find it. Such was the power of physical desire. In a very real way I realized we don't have physical pleasures, they have us. We would be enslaved to the satisfaction of our desires until we were freed of the trap of the ego-personality. This clearly was how I had lived and how most of humanity lived.

The Divine experience, on the other hand, left me feeling completely enlivened, continuously full, blissfully complete and ever new without end. Desire did not exist in the Divine inner kingdom, only total fulfillment and unending bliss. I could hardly believe my great, good fortune. I had made it out of the endless sea of desire and into the kingdom of Divinity. I crossed over! I felt so free. I had no idea a person could feel so free. It was a whole other world.

As I looked across the lawn, on this day of Self-Realization, I noticed the leaves, the buildings, the dirt, indeed the very air sparkled like diamonds. I could see tiny particles of Light in each. It reminded me of the experience I had had in my backyard in 1984. This scintillating Light was in everything, everywhere I looked. But now, I understood in a much deeper way, that everything in this world was made of consciousness whether animate or inanimate. And this consciousness was Divine Light, Divinity itself, God made manifest as the world. This was the experience that sages, mystics and saints had spoken of so many times. And now, in this moment, I knew it as Truth.

I saw some people walking along the sidewalk crossing from one building to the next and I could hardly believe my eyes! Hovering about 37° above each of their foreheads was an oval-shaped disc of light, and coming from it were Light particles flowing down over each person like a shower of snowflakes. They reminded me of walking Christmas trees with the lighted star at the top and the light draping down over the tree. I had an urge to shout "Look, look just above your eyes, it's your Soul! Can't you see it?" But I knew they couldn't and it would not matter if I had shouted it. They still would not be able to see it. But I wanted so much for them to see it. I was in an ecstatic, blissful state of Divinity. I felt so fulfilled, so complete, so satisfied, so immensely, completely happy. And I felt totally grateful.

This state I knew was my true state and yet I could remember the state of living in the ego-personality. I remembered it didn't feel like living at all. The ego-personality state felt like the walking dead. When God said, "This is the Living Presence. This is Living. This is real," I understood these words as a direct experience. This was indeed true living. All my suffering, emotional, spiritual, mental and physical pain had left me, along with desire and fear. There was nothing else to achieve, nothing else to strive for. I was elated and also completely aware of all of my surroundings. I wasn't spaced out or unable to function. In fact, I was more present than I had ever been in my life and acutely aware of everything going on around me. I felt so completely grounded, whole and unafraid. It was the most relaxing state I had ever experienced. Finally, I was home, at last. "My God," I thought, "I didn't even know this place inside me even existed." Heaven was indeed inside me. I kept thanking God. Finally, no more suffering.

Living on this Earth in the world, I had known a lot about suffering, either experiencing it myself or reading or hearing about other people's suffering. I had accepted suffering as a part of life. I had no idea that one could actually live in this world without suffering. I had always accepted that human beings would suffer one way or the other. No one had told me of the bliss of the Self. No one had ever told me that bliss was our True state. Most of humanity believed we could only live in the human realm, in the human state of consciousness, belonging to human beings and human suffering, with God being somewhere else. But on this day I knew we were more than human beings, we were Divinity itself. I knew suffering would eventually leave with the dawn of our Divinity in the same way that darkness gives way to the rising sun.

I looked across the lawn. What I saw astonished me. I could hardly believe the sight. About thirty feet off the ground I saw what could only be called a vision. A cloud appeared with it Jesus standing in the middle of it. His hands and eyes were lifted towards the heavens. The cloud along with Jesus began ascending until it disappeared. "Oh," I wondered, "Have I too ascended?" Is this the ascension we are all to make, ascending from human consciousness to Divine consciousness?" I felt this was true.

This day was a shattering day for me. All my concepts of people, life, suffering and God were shattered, completely blown apart with no trace of recognition. On that day, I saw the greatness of humanity. I experienced "the Divinity that awaits all Mankind" and nothing would ever be the same for me. All my judgments and criticisms of others and myself were shattered. No longer could I judge anyone and let myself get away with it. Divinity lived in everyone and everything, so who was there to judge, who was there to criticize? This Divinity was void of any kind of exclusiveness; it belonged to everyone, everywhere, equally without judgment or measure. To behave or believe otherwise would be to deny our very own existence.

I truly knew that a new day was dawning for humanity—a new opportunity was being revealed and offered. It was nothing short of astonishing. It was real and it was big. I felt the end of our limited existence, as we knew it, was coming. For thousands of years, the masses of humanity had been suffering and living under the weight of the ego-personality. We had been in a long sleep regarding our true, normal state of Divinity. But a new day would come with the dawning of our Divinity. I knew with certainty that each of us, if we wanted and if we chose, could wake up to this.

My experience of Divinity continued as I watched people walking by. Not only could I see their Divinity pouring over their physical bodies, I also saw their struggles to be free, their issues and concerns. I thought, "Did they know they were God in the midst of these struggles?" I also felt enormous love for each person. It was difficult to describe the kind of love I felt. It had none of the impurities of human love such as lust, possessiveness, infatuation, attachment or jealousy. This love loved because it's nature was love. It was an unsullied love.

I looked down at my watch, realizing I needed to go and help with the lunch dishes as part of my service while staying at the retreat. What an interesting situation. There I was in the state of Divinity knowing I was God and I needed to do the dishes! I realized my state was the thing that made all the difference while living in human form. I realized that we didn't just sit around doing nothing when we became Self-Realized. We still functioned. But we functioned in continual joy and bliss. In fact, it didn't matter what you were doing in this state of bliss. The state didn't come and go. It remained what it was. We didn't lose our minds in all this, we gained our Divinity and functioned with greater clarity and concern for the welfare of others.

As I got up to walk to the dishroom, I knew I was experiencing the highest state a human could attain. I knew there was nothing else for me to attain. This was it. This knowing continued to overwhelm me with gratitude and an enormous peace.

Still in this state, I stood in the dishroom in front of a huge tub filled with soapsuds and dirty dishes. I wondered what effect my state had on those around me who were also washing dishes. As I had that thought, I looked up. At the same time, a woman across from me looked directly into my eyes. As our eyes met, she burst into tears. I quickly looked down into the soapy dishwater as I heard her sobs. The force of this God love was so palpable inside my body that I knew she felt it when I looked at her. I knew as she sobbed that this love inside me had touched that source of love within her. Her tears were tears of longing for the Divinity living inside herself. I finished the dishes in silence and kept my eyes on the soapsuds from then on.

As I walked out of the dishroom some twenty minutes later, I wasn't prepared for what was to happen next. I noticed my state was beginning to slip. Someone stopped to ask me a question. As I slipped out of my state of total union with God, the first feeling I experienced was fear! I quickly answered their question and left the building. I could feel the veil of fear closing over my state of total blissful union with God. I could feel my old ego-driven personality state, with all of its feeling of lack, seep back into my awareness. "Oh no, please don't make me go back! Don't make me go back!" That thought screamed through my mind. I felt desperate.

I realized very quickly that I was now back in my old human consciousness state of feeling imperfect, small and fearful. What a plight! I was in spiritual agony. I felt exiled from my true home of God-Realization, Self-Realization. The bliss and ecstasy were gone. I ran over to a wooded area, where I could sob. I wanted to wail, but felt constrained by not wanting to call attention to myself and disturb others on the grounds. What would I say anyway? How would I explain what had happened? "Oh, I was God-Realized but I had to go back?" I was afraid they would not understand, and to me, that would be even worse than keeping it to myself.

Was this what falling from Grace was all about? Was this the so-called 'original sin': forgetting that we were God, that we were all One with God? I felt this was true. Agony is the only word I know that could even begin to approach what I felt. Why did I have to go back to mere human consciousness when Divine consciousness was my true and natural state? What cruel fate was this?

I wondered why I had to return to the ego-state after experiencing the bliss of Self-Realization. The only plausible answer had to be karma. I simply had more karma that had to be lived out and experienced. I was beside myself with grief. I could barely comfort myself as I felt the torture of my own thoughts. "This is hell enough," I thought, "Feeling separate from God." But even in this depth of agony of returning to my ego state of consciousness, came the enormous gratitude I felt for knowing beyond any shadow of a doubt, that Self-Realization was the destiny of mankind. And of particular importance to me, I knew it was my destiny as well.

In my agony of having to return to the state of separation, I knew I wanted more than anything to return to that state of Divinity, my natural state. I wished that every person would come to experience that state for at least a few moments, so that they would know the possibility that existed inside them. But on this day in July of 1988, I could not remain in the state of Self-Realization; instead, I had to return to the human consciousness of the ego-personality.

A few years later, I was introduced to a poem by Hafiz entitled, *In a Tree House*. It truly spoke to my experience of the moment of being opened to Self-Realization:

In A Tree House
Light
Will someday split you open
Even if your life is now a cage,
For a Divine seed, the crown of destiny,
Is hidden and sown on an ancient, fertile plain
You hold the title to.
Love will surely bust you wide open

Into an unfettered, blooming new galaxy,
Even if your mind is now a spoiled mule.

A life-giving radiance will come,
The Friend's gratuity will come -
O look again within yourself,
For I know you were once the elegant host
To all the marvels in creation.

From a sacred crevice in your body
A bow rises each night
And shoots your soul into God.

Behold the Beautiful Drunk Singing One
From the lunar vantage point of love.
He is conducting the affairs
Of the whole universe
While throwing wild parties
In a tree house - on a limb
In your heart. [2]

2From *The Subject Tonight is Love, 60 Wild & Sweet Poems of Hafiz,*
copyright 1996 & 2003 by Daniel Ladinsky and used by his permission.

Chapter 17

RETURNING HOME

When I returned home from the retreat I was still reeling from my experience of Self-Realization. I was trying to integrate that experience with my life, which was filled with uncertainties and ambiguities. I tried to share the powerful transformation that had happened to me but no one seemed to be able to grasp its import. Finally, I realized they could not understand what they had never experienced.

I felt spiritually lonely when I realized no one else I knew had had this experience of Self-Realization. Over time I discovered that this experience was not commonplace, even amongst those who had been on a spiritual path for years. I had thought that if it happened to me, it must have happened to others who had been on a path for much longer than myself. I wondered why I had come to Self-Realization relatively early in my spiritual life.

When I wrote to my teacher about it, she said it was because of my faith in the spiritual energy within myself. She also had someone call me three times, a week apart to give me the message that this was a great experience. I was so grateful for these calls, as I knew for sure that my teacher understood completely what others could not validate.

I continued writing spiritual poetry as it was a source of comfort and a way for me to express the depth of the experiences I had been given. The poems more easily captured that which was difficult for me to express in any other form. The following poems came directly out of my Self-Realization experience:

Humanity
Oh Humanity,
If for one brief moment
you could experience
That Greatness within,
The Earth
would become a Sun
and the warmth of its rays
would bring tears
to the eyes of God.

A Thousand Suns
A Thousand Suns shining
coming out of the Darkness
In what seemed like forever,
calling me home.

A Thousand Suns blazing,
A Thousand Drums drumming,
calling me home
calling me home.

And if I go,
I'll never come back,
I'll never be the same,
I'll never be the same.

And if I go,
I'll never come back,
I'll never be the same,
I'll never be the same.

Live
*Give up all
that you know,
That you may Live.*

God's Little Trumpet
*Long before the first strains
of morning's light
The sparrow's song tells
of today's miracle to come.
Listen, oh listen
to their melodic calls and
Hail the One
to whom they sing.
Like God's little trumpet,
Sing praises to the Lord.*

Mystery of Grace
*Oh Mystery of Grace
shed your Light on me,
For you alone
Yes, you alone
can come and set me free.
Not pleaful words
nor things I do
can shed the shackles here,
Not thoughtful gifts
nor handmade tricks
or other things I fear.
Oh Mystery, Oh Mystery
Oh Mystery of Grace,
Shine on me, Oh Shine on me
and with your sweet embrace,
Free this Soul and Free this Heart
to be as pure as you,
So I can fly on treetops high
And Live each day in you.*

I went back to work as usual, but nothing was as usual inside. Now I knew for certain that Self-Realization was the goal of this life. It was no longer a concept or something I had read and understood intellectually. For me, it was now the Truth. I realized most people were too caught up in the buzz and glitz of the world to even care about getting free from it. I was caught up in the world wishing I could be free from it. I didn't mean free from it as in dying and leaving this Earth, I meant free on the inside from attachments and aversions.

I knew I needed to continue confronting the issues in my life as Mary. Only then would I discover the freedom inherent in being fully awake in the present moment. I continued to feel I was living on a fast spiritual track and that I hadn't a moment to waste. Karmic experiences came and went. Sometimes it felt hard and sometimes it felt easy. Every time, I felt challenged and changed by them. I had to keep learning to let go of things when they were outmoded and be willing to move on. Amongst all the commotion of the life I had been thrown back into upon arriving home, I kept remembering my experience of Self-Realization and would end up in tears. I so yearned to be "home" again in what I now considered the normal state, that of Self-Realization, rather than in the fearful, ego-driven personality. But I knew I had unfinished business, unfinished karma that had to be lived out. Yet, that was sore comfort.

A month later, in August, my teenage daughter, Deborah who up to now wondered what meditation was all about, decided to come with me on a weekend retreat. It was an amazing experience for both of us. I watched her soul wake up to its beauty when she met the Self-Realized monk. I saw the same Light in my daughter's face, that I had experienced in my own. It was as if someone had turned on a light switch inside her and she woke up to her inner Truth of Divinity. She too had received a spiritual awakening.

This awakening had an amazing impact on her. When she returned home her school grades went from "Cs" and

"Ds, to "As" and "Bs". On one parent night, her science teacher pulled me aside and wanted to know what happened to her. I told him about the retreat my daughter had been on. He said she was like a completely new person. She was taking responsibility in class and acting like a leader. I was amazed and delighted. Of course, life did continue to present challenges but the inner door she walked through opened her forever. I felt so proud of all the changes she was making and truly joyful for her.

Chapter 18

DEATH

The fall came quickly. It was now October 1988, just a few short months since my experience of Self-Realization. I maintained my daily practice of reading sacred texts and meditating. As I had mentioned, I loved meditating outside during lunch, but in the fall and winter, when it was too cold, I would meditate on a bench in the lobby of the Electrical Engineering building at MIT, where I worked. The lobby had big glass windows on all sides and faced Massachusetts Avenue, a busy street. As I sat on the bench, this day in early October, my back leaning against a wall, eating my sandwich, I was reading an article from a spiritual magazine recounting some experiences people had with the teacher of my teacher, who passed in 1982. He too was a Self-Realized monk. They talked about how when he entered the room, they would feel so much love coming from him, like a huge ocean of love washing over them and they would burst into tears. Another said he could hear inner sounds inside himself, like the wind from a tornado or hurricane. Another heard the sound of a conch shell blowing like a trumpet. The experiences varied like this.

I had heard of these inner sounds that resided in our consciousness, but I had not experienced them. I read about this monk saint with genuine fascination and awe and with the yearning to have been in his presence. Surprisingly, I found tears rolling down my face since I realized this could never happen given his passing. I would have to be satisfied with reading about what it was like to meet him, instead of having that experience myself.

Resigned to that thought, I put the magazine down and closed my eyes to meditate. My back rested against the wall as I sat in a relaxed cross-legged position. With my eyes closed, I focused on my breath, slowly breathing in and out. A few people walked by through the lobby, talking as they made their way outside.

After about ten minutes, I heard someone speaking to me. He said, "Are you ready?" Thinking this was just some student walking by trying to bother me, I ignored him and kept my eyes closed. A moment passed. Again the voice said, "Are you ready?" This time, with my eyes still closed, I turned my attention to the voice, which came from the left side where I was sitting. I could not believe it. I saw the monk I had been reading about approaching! "My God," I thought, "I'm having one of those spiritual experiences I've heard people talk about where people actually see someone in meditation as if in real life with their eyes open!" I could hardly believe what was happening to me. My eyes were closed, but I saw him as if they were open.

As the monk got close to my left side, he turned and started walking away from me, directly in front of me. Then he stopped and turned around. He then walked straight towards me and when he got very close, he became the swirling energy form of the Milky Way! His energy form as the Milky Way entered my solar plexus just above my navel. Immediately, I began hearing many inner sounds from nature. This astounded me.

First, I heard the sound of a hurricane with loud winds whirling around. It was so loud! Then I heard conches trumpeting and then the sound of a tornado and a locomotive. Next, I heard the sound of the ocean and then all of the sounds blended together with bells ringing and the intense sound of whirling wind. I felt some of the energy go down into my legs, but the majority of it started to move up from my solar plexus and into my chest region and then around my shoulders.

The sound got louder and louder until it reached my eardrums. At that point, I thought, "If this continues, my eardrums will burst!" Just as I had that thought, I also realized that I was about to leave my body, to die! Then, I thought, "But who will take care of my daughter Deborah?" Just then, I heard a calming voice say that I did not have to worry, everything would be fine. With that reassurance, I truly felt that everything would fine and I let myself relax into the experience. The whole energy of my body gathered together and left out the top of my head, in a loud gust of wind.

In an instant, I traveled from my physical body on Earth to some place in space. At some point, a few seconds later, I saw, not with the eyes of the physical body, but with my body of consciousness, two rectangular windows of Light, each the size of a regular window in a house, one located directly above the other. As I gazed at these windows of Light, I felt very drawn to go through them. I somehow knew that if I entered those windows, I would not return to where I had been. The Light felt like a magnetic pull of love drawing me to it. It felt so peaceful and enormously comforting. Just at that moment, the thought came again, "But what about Deborah?" But the magnet of love drawing me was too strong to resist and I could not help but move towards it. As I moved forward, the monk touched my left side to stop me and said, "Not yet." I understood that I had to return to where I had been. But where was that anyway? I could not really remember. I wondered how I would get back, since I didn't know the way. Then, I looked down and what I saw was amazing.

As I gazed downward, I saw a silver cord that looked like a filament of Light about one-eighth inch in diameter, connected to the solar plexus area of my Light body of consciousness, just above where the naval of my physical body would be located. This cord was flexible and very, very long, extending downward, as far as I could see. It had a lot of slack in it and floated loosely in the air. I realized that it was my job to go back to where I had been. To do that, I found I needed to concentrate very hard on following the silver cord. Simultaneously, I also remembered something I had read in Shirley MacLaine's book, "Out on a Limb". She spoke about her experience of the silver cord when she was meditating in a cave in Peru. In the book, Shirley told of how she had left her physical body while meditating and saw the silver cord as she floated away from her body. As she floated higher and higher, she became frightened and immediately she was back in her body. I thought, "Oh my God, Shirley isn't crazy after all, here's the silver cord she spoke about!"

In the beginning, as I focused on following the cord, I saw only the cord and nothing else. It took all my strength to stay focused on it. But then, all of a sudden, the vista opened in front of me and revealed our entire solar system! It was at that point I realized wherever I was going back to was very far from where I had just been, when viewing the windows of Light. I could see the silver cord extending all the way in front of me, far ahead. At this point, I could not tell which planet I would be going to, but as I followed the cord, I realized I was going to planet Earth.

As I zoomed by the other planets, and got closer to the Earth, I realized I was going to North America. Zooming in further, I realized I was going to the United States. Zooming further down, I saw Massachusetts and then the town of Cambridge and then the Electrical Engineering building at MIT. At that point, I went through the roof of the building and was floating up by the ceiling looking down at a body meditating on a bench that had the silver cord connected to it at the top of its head. I remember thinking, "So that's the body I have to go back to." It was then I realized that I had not known if I were going into a female or male body; that was how detached I felt from that body or any body for that matter.

I felt totally like me in this spirit state of consciousness and felt no attachment whatsoever to the physical body I was looking at sitting on the bench. Then I followed the silver cord all the way and entered the top of the head and finally felt my "spirit Self" slip inside the physical body. When I had fully entered, the body actually jumped a little with a thud. "Ouch," I thought. I felt as if I had entered a tight shoe. It was so confining!

At some point, I became aware of the mind and physical karma connected to this incarnation. "Oh no," I thought, "What was I going to do? How would I ever get free of these issues, these tendencies?" As I immersed myself in these rather desperate thoughts, suddenly the monk's face appeared right in front of mine! I could hardly believe it. My eyes were still closed, but there he was again, as real as life. He said, "The veil is very thin between here and there, very thin." Then suddenly he disappeared!

"My God!" I thought, "What had happened?" I was sure with this racket going on inside me, I had attracted the attention of every passerby who happened to wander through the lobby at the time. But as I opened my eyes, no one was there.

Immediately I thought, "Wow, you really can see and hear without the physical body." I realized you could actually see and hear with your consciousness; you did not need a physical body to do that. But if you were using a physical body, you needed to have your eyes intact and functioning properly so the energy could work through them. I realized the actual power behind seeing rested with one's consciousness. That meant that sight was one of the innate powers within consciousness.

And another more important thing, I realized I had just been given the experience of death! I experienced the dropping away of the physical body was not the end of our existence. We had a big misunderstanding about what we called death. The body didn't die, because it was never alive to begin with. It just had the *appearance* of being alive.

The body was a temporary puppet of the life force of consciousness. It was a housing for the Light. It was a temple for the Light of consciousness. I understood this Light contained abilities, knowledge and wisdom all in itself and it was not confined to time or space or to a physical body. It could travel anywhere. I wondered if that was the way people could do distant viewing. I felt that was true.

I reflected, "If the physical body was never alive to begin with and only the Light of consciousness which filled it was, and we couldn't die, then there was no death! Therefore, only consciousness was alive and it never died!" For me, on that day, death itself died. Death was always a subject I feared and wondered about. But that day, I knew for certain, there was no such thing as death. You didn't die; you couldn't die, not ever! The you that was really you as consciousness could not die. To say that you lived forever was quite true.

"Wait a minute," I thought, "If you couldn't die and were never dead, then how could you be born? Oh my God, birth did not exist either, because how could we be born, if we never died!" I realized in that moment that if there was nothing but consciousness and different states of consciousness, then when we vacate our physical body, we would pass on with the same state of consciousness. In other words, right now if we left this body, whatever state of awareness we were in, we would continue to be in that state until we got another body in another incarnation to develop our awareness even more. These incarnations would continue until we reached the zenith of human awareness: Self-Realization. Then the cycle of birth and death would no longer be necessary. The cycle of karma would be broken and no longer would we need to live in disunion.

No wonder the spiritual masters urged us to wake up now and not to waste this life in just material pursuits. We were here to remember who we were. That was the whole point of coming here. I remembered reading that it was not very easy to achieve a human birth and because of that we should not waste it.

So many thoughts and understandings whirled about in my mind as I sat there on the bench looking out onto Massachusetts Avenue. Truly I could not believe my good fortune in being given this most incredible experience and all the knowledge that came with it. What a great time for me! I realized that the fear of death no longer existed for me as death itself had fled in the wake of my new understanding.

I realized it seemed so natural to completely identify with this physical body as myself. If I hadn't had the experience of my own Soul as the real me, I could not have made the distinction. It was all so convincing while living in a body, that the physical body was the only reality.

I also understood that even though there was no death, there was the process of letting go or "dropping away" of the physical body. Could I make the process easier if I identified myself as my Soul, as consciousness, rather than as my physical body? Could it be that my consciousness could just leave through the top of the head as I had just experienced? I felt so. If so, then it would be important for me to be more identified as consciousness, to connect with my Divinity fully while still in this physical body on Earth.

I thought that in the not so distant future, as people came more in union with themselves as consciousness, they could be conscious participants in allowing themselves to pass out of their bodies simply by being more identified as consciousness while alive. Death, the passing out from this physical body, was something we would all experience. It would be the last thing we did on this Earth, yet it seemed to be the last thing we ever talked about. I thought meditation could be taught with the understanding that one could make the connection with the Self and in doing so make passing out of the body easier by focusing on the Self. I imagined if we knew for certain that we lived forever, then the fear of death would lose its grip on humanity and it would become more important *how* we lived each day. "Oh my," I thought, "There truly is no escape from bad behavior, as we live for all eternity and where we end up after we drop the body is dependent on *how* we live!" This I knew for certain. It was better to live a life with the understanding that God lived in me and in everyone and to behave accordingly. For me, this was a sobering thought as it meant I had to live in a very conscious way in every moment.

I reflected on how our being here on Earth was a temporary visit. The Earth and our physical bodies were temporary hotels. It could take many lifetimes to live out our desires until one day these desires dried up with the dawn of Self-Realization.

Having had this experience of death as I sat in the lobby at work, I had a greater appreciation for life. I knew without any doubt that the sole purpose for taking on a body, for taking on a human birth was to experience Self-Realization. Self-Realization was simply a part of a human's evolution. With my new understanding of death, I no longer feared it; and life itself took on a greater significance and the importance of living fully in the moment became more real and meaningful.

My lunchtime had stretched into an hour as all of these understandings washed over me, one after another. This great experience of death felt so natural. I remembered that I had read somewhere that a yogi could experience his own death while still alive. I had always wondered what that meant and how that would be possible. Now I knew for myself.

I went back to my office feeling changed inwardly. I could hardly wait to talk to some of my friends who were also on the same spiritual path about what had happened. I wondered if they had had this experience too, but had never felt comfortable sharing it. As I shared my amazing experience of death with a few close friends, I discovered that indeed no one else I knew had ever had this experience.

I realized it was a time for me to once again immerse myself in the practices of meditation, service, and contemplation rather than trying to share what I had experienced. Perhaps that would come at another time.

For now, I knew I still had much to resolve in myself. I also had a sense that much more was to come. I continued on with my life trying to incorporate all the lessons.

Chapter 19

MOTHER MEETS THE MONK

It was now 1990, two years after my daughter, Deborah met the monk. I was sitting in my mother's apartment having lunch and I said, "Hey Mom, would you like to do something different this summer?" She said, "Sure, I was feeling like I'd like to try something different." When I asked her if she would like to come with her granddaughter and me to meet the monk we had been talking about the last few years, she said, "Yes."

Finally the day came. I had been at the retreat site with my daughter for the past week. I left my daughter at the retreat while I went to pick up my mother. It was raining very heavily like a monsoon. When I arrived back at the retreat, I met my daughter at the front door as planned. There were hundreds of people around. I realized that the monk was in a receiving room just off the main lobby. My daughter greeted us with the message that the monk would be meeting the three of us together. I was amazed, as it was unusual to have personal meetings with the monk apart from the crowd.

As we waited on a bench among hundreds of people who

had arrived by then, I wondered at my mother's great good fortune to be having a private meeting with the Self-Realized monk as her first introduction. I thought perhaps I had underestimated my mother!

As the three of us walked forward, with my mother in between my daughter and myself, our arms entwined, the monk said, "Three generations." I thought it was such a blessing to have three generations in the company of an enlightened one who could awaken one's innate Divinity and provide spiritual guidance.

As we grew closer, my mother leaned over and handed the monk something. "What could that be?" I thought. I didn't even see my mother carrying anything. How strange. With that, the monk said with great joy, "For me?" My mother answered with a simple, "Yes." As she handed a beautiful hand-sewn white, silk heart-shaped pillow to the monk, the monk pulled my mother towards her embracing her with great love saying, "Grandmother." I stood in awe over the entire sight. My mother was being received with the same pure respect she so clearly showed the monk.

My mother was soon offered a chair, while my daughter and I sat on the floor in front of the monk. Then the monk turned to my mother and said, "You brought the rain." By then, I began to question my opinion of my mother, as rain can be considered a sign of great blessings and clearly the monk was acknowledging my mother's presence as one who brought blessings. That had a profound effect on me and I felt a shift inside myself regarding my mother. I could feel a subtle emotional wall begin to soften. This was a wall that had always been there after she left the family when I was just eleven. It was clear that a deep healing was being bestowed upon our family. But that wasn't the end of it.

All of a sudden, the monk leaned forward toward me, looking right into my eyes and said, "Only one daughter?" "Why was she bringing this up now?" I thought. I knew she was aware that I had two daughters, one sitting by my side from my marriage and one I had given up for adoption over twenty-five years ago, because I had written to her about them in the past. Her words penetrated and reverberated in my being. I was so astonished I was unable to speak. My daughter answered, "Yes, only me." In my mind, I kept saying, "I have two, I have two," but my mouth could not speak. Then the conversation shifted as the monk sat back in her chair. The meeting went on and after fifteen minutes, we were ushered out of the room with a gift of chocolates.

After the meeting, I was obsessed with thinking about the daughter I had given up for adoption. What did this mean that the monk brought up the subject? Would we be reunited soon? I hoped so. I decided I would ask the monk about my adopted daughter at the public program that would be held in a few days.

The day of the program arrived. When the time came in the program to see the monk for a few moments, I asked her about my daughter. She put up her hand, as if in a blessing, and I knew that everything would be alright and that I would be reunited with my daughter some day. I had only a glimpse of her after giving birth in a hospital in Canada so many years ago and I had never gotten a chance to hold her.

When I returned home, my relationship with my youngest daughter and my mother continued to improve. I also tied up loose ends with old friendships, so that I could move on.

I had a very powerful dream shortly after returning home that clarified my relationship with the monk. In the dream, I was in a heavenly place. There was a soft bluish light spread everywhere and I noticed that there was no sun and no moon. I wondered from where the light was coming. I looked out onto a completely flat terrain. There were hundreds of people seated three feet apart on the ground in meditation. They were wrapped in white shawls and robes and they were completely still. The silence was palpable. All of a sudden a man stood up who was also wrapped in a white shawl. I knew I was to be given a place to sit and meditate. As I had that thought, the man gestured for me to sit on the ground.

As I started to sit down, a laser-like beam of white light

appeared, aimed at my heart. I looked out and saw the light beam coming from somewhere. I followed the light beam to its source. There in front of me, sitting on a chair on a low platform surrounded with others in white shawls and robes, was Jesus, also shrouded in a white robe. I could hardly believe my eyes. I immediately knelt down in front of him. His eyes were blue, his skin olive, his full beard and long hair were brown in color.

I felt heartbroken and upset wondering where he had been all this time; I had missed him so much. I looked deeply into His eyes. In my upset at Him for leaving, I said with angry tears in my eyes and pain in my heart, "You promised me fulfillment." He looked into my eyes with so much love. I felt his compassionate love enter my heart. Tears rolled down my cheeks as my anger melted into a profound love for Him. I could feel myself merging with His Divine energy. Just then his face began to disappear and in its place was the face of my teacher monk. I immediately understood that my teacher was here to complete the promise of fulfillment that Jesus had made to me so many years ago.

When I awoke I was amazed. The dream felt completely real and I knew beyond any shadow of doubt that I had actually met Jesus in a spiritual realm. His love felt like a soothing balm. I also felt so grateful to be in the company of the Self-Realized monk to complete my spiritual journey on Earth to be fulfilled in spirit through Self-Realization.

Chapter 20

CREATION

A year passed and in the summer of 1991, I found myself at a kind of spiritual standstill. Friends of mine had signed up for a self-improvement course and invited me to attend, which I did.

The course was described as an intense four-day event, from 8 am to 9 pm, focusing on uncovering and clearing away recurring mental and emotional patterns that kept a person stuck in their life. I figured it would be great to be in an environment with a group of people all focused on the same desire to release old patterns. There was no spiritual content to the course, but rather a philosophical one in how to live one's life more fully.

When I first signed up for the workshop, inwardly I asked for my teacher's blessings so that whatever needed to be revealed would be revealed so that I could live in union with God. Having invoked Grace, I went to my first class. These classes proved very demanding. There were individual shares, group shares with ten people and shares with the entire group, which consisted of about two-hundred people.

It was the afternoon of the third day and we were all gathered in a room. The entire group was sharing together. One woman spoke about her past experience of being physically assaulted. The experience was one of great pain for her. Clearly she was still struggling with trying to process this event, which happened many years ago. The instructor began to speak about looking at this event from a different point of view, a more detached point of view. She said that we usually look at things from a perspective of some event being either good or bad. "But," she said, "What if you looked at an event, not as being either inherently good or bad, but just as an event." The woman, of course, balked at this thought, as I would have, had it happened to me.

The instructor pressed on to bring her point across. She said, "You know some people might say that that event wasn't bad, some might say it was good, at least from the standpoint that the event started you looking at your entire life differently. You say that you developed more compassion for others after it happened. So some might say what happened was good, while you feel and others might say what happened was bad. Do you see what I am saying? An event happened and someone labeled it bad and someone else labeled it good depending on their viewpoint. But perhaps, it was neither good nor bad. Perhaps it could be looked at as just an event."

Just then a man in the group stood up. He said, "It sounds like you are talking about the void." He went on to say that the spiritual void is a state of nothingness, just a neutral state of being.

Up until now, I was sitting in my chair listening to this very interesting philosophical discussion. But something unbelievable happened when he said the word void. As he spoke the word, I was given an experience of the void!

As I sat in my chair, I experienced a bolt of lightning, shooting from the heavens, that went right through the top of my head all the way down my spine! With that, my whole consciousness was thrown into the void. I, my consciousness, experienced being in a very deep, black, velvety outer space. Although all I saw was black, the void had a Presence in it: it wasn't empty. It was the Presence of the deepest, most silent love. It was God.

Just then I saw the huge mouth of God, which measured the size of the heavens. God's mouth was wide open and out of it spilled all kinds of forms: vegetables, trees, plants, animals and it went on and on. It reminded me of a gigantic cornucopia! At the same time, I heard a sound, the sound of Om (Aum). It was a constant sound, recurring over and over again in the background, like a drone. I had an immediate understanding that this sound of Om was going on all the time all around me everywhere and that it had no beginning and it had no end. I understood that Om was the sound of God and the feeling associated with God was Divine Love.

I realized that this sound was occurring all the time, all around us, but we didn't hear it. I had read that some had heard it in meditation, just as I was hearing it now. I also felt God as an emanating energy of Divine Love. The sound of Om was this Divine Love and it pulsed all around me and in me. I realized that the whole world had been created from this Om and was being continually created, transformed, maintained and destroyed and re-created again in an endless cycle. That meant that every moment was being recreated and that nothing stayed the same. I understood that all the galaxies were suspended and held in place by this vibrational force of God. This vibrational force was like a divine glue. Everything floated in and was held together by this constant Om, including us! I understood that since we were God, our vibrational consciousness was also made of Om. Everything, including us, was consciousness and consciousness was Light, and Light was a wave-vibration, and every wave-vibration had a sound and that sound was Om.

I knew that sound, light and love were all wave vibrations of energy and this was what our Divine Consciousness was made of: Om. If we were Om, then we too created using

Om. I thought about our creative process: first we had a desire for something, then we thought about creating it, then we talked about creating it and then we actually made it appear. All of that came from a thought vibration called an idea. We opened our mouths like God and out came the blueprint for a creation from an idea. Of course, the process took us a little longer since most of us were not in perfect union with our Godness. But if we were, things would happen almost instantly.

Some speak of the void as nothing, but I experienced it as the No-thing and it wasn't nothing, it was something. It was God and the feeling of it was love.

The experience and understanding of the void all seemed to happen in a split second. When my consciousness went back to normal, I jumped up from my chair and shouted, "I've got it!" As I shouted that, I felt so much love emanating from me and in particular, from my third eye chakra, between my eyes. There was a beacon of Light pouring from it, much like a miner's light on a helmet that goes around the head in order to see inside caves. I felt ablaze with love and very peaceful.

The teacher said, "What, what have you got?" I couldn't believe that I jumped up like that. That wasn't like me. What was I going to say? So I stammered out something like, "Love, there is only love all around, the no-thing is not nothing, it's love." My revelation was greeted with silence as people looked at me rather quizzically. I sat down. The teacher continued with her dialogue.

Shortly afterwards, the class took a break. As I was waiting in line in the ladies bathroom, I still felt the Light pouring from my head and I felt the love. When I looked at myself in the mirror, I could see Light coming from my head and face. I was quite amazed at this and felt very fortunate to be in this state. Someone next to me mentioned that I looked different. Some ventured to ask what happened to me. "Oh," I said, "I experienced that all there is is love, all around, nothing but love." I didn't quite know what else to say and it seemed neither did they. I was happy when the class officially ended that day so I could be by myself at home in this state of love and contentment.

At home, I could revel in this state of peace and love uninterrupted. My mind was so quiet and still. It wasn't thinking its usually self-deprecating thoughts that seemed to have a life of their own and played like background music. Instead, I was in a state of being free from hardly any thoughts and in a state of happiness. As I sat in my kitchen, I had the experience of my mind as a black box hovering next to my head. It was a construct of energy in which I could have thoughts and use these thoughts as needed to manage information useful in interacting with the world. I realized that I didn't have to have any thoughts at all if I didn't want to. In that case, I would just be in my natural state of blissful being and contentment. I realized that most of my life had been spent being the victim of my own mind, unable to control the thoughts that constantly flowed through it, mostly with self-doubt and self-deprecation. I understood with great clarity, that this was the state of most of mankind.

I remembered reading about the advice from sages that said that you should have one less thought a day until you had no thoughts at all—so it must be possible, as I was experiencing something very close to that state and I liked it a whole lot.

When I looked in the mirror, the Light continued to pour from my forehead as I maintained the state. I relished this state, hoping it would last forever. Although it didn't, I got to live in it for twenty-four hours and once again, I was given a glimpse into the Divine state of consciousness that lived inside.

When I returned to my normal state, once again the many thoughts of self-deprecation and self-doubt returned. I wasn't so dismayed by this, as I understood one day, when the time was right, I would return to my natural state of Divine consciousness. One day I knew I would be free of the self- deprecating state of the ego-mind-personality.

Chapter 21

THE REUNION

A few more years went by and in 1994 my father passed. I was so glad that I had had time to see him before he left his body. In a letter a few months beforehand, I expressed all the love and appreciation I had for him. A month after he passed he came to me in a dream to let me know he was doing well and he seemed very happy.

With his passing, my father made it possible for me to take a trip to India to see my teacher once again and to study. A few months after my return from India, I got a phone call from a social worker. As soon as she announced she was a social worker, I knew it was a call about my daughter, the one I gave up for adoption. The social worker wanted to know if I wanted to talk with her. I had named my daughter Margaret. My immediate answer was yes! A stream of questions came pouring out of me. "How is she? What's her name? Where does she live? Is she okay?" The social worker told me her adoptive parents named her Cindy and that she lived in New Jersey.

After I hung up from the social worker I awaited Cindy's

call. In a few moments the phone rang. When I picked up the phone and said hello I heard my daughter's voice for the first time. "Hello Mary?" "Yes." "Mom?" "Yes!" She started crying. Her voice sounded so much like mine that I was taken back. We made plans for a reunion in a month. When I got off the phone I was in a state of emotional numbness. It took me a few days to realize this numbness was what was covering over all the feelings I had about leaving my daughter behind in Canada. To help with this transition I found a support group who worked with reunions of this kind. This gave me an opportunity to work through some of the profound grief and lack of self-worth I felt surrounding the relinquishment of my baby. The day I was to travel to see Cindy, I felt the grief well up inside me. It was so intense that I fell to my knees in sorrow and began to sob. How was I ever going to be able to process all this? How was I ever going to forgive myself? I felt terrible about myself for walking away from my baby. It didn't matter that I had no real choice at the time.

I needed to pull myself together if I was going to be able to drive four hours in the car to where I would be reunited with her. I called out to God, "Please God help me!" Just then the phone rang! I was surprised that I picked it up since I was still crying. There on the phone was a very dear friend of mine, Aditi. She immediately said, "Mary, how are you?" As I caught my breath, I told her what was going on and how I called out to God for help. She said, "That's why I'm calling!" "What?" I said in disbelief. She said, "Last night I was awakened at two in the morning with a poem writing itself in my mind. I could not go back to sleep until I wrote it down. It's about you and Cindy. I knew you would be leaving soon to see her. I didn't know it was today but I knew I had to call you right away and read the poem to you. I know it was from God. He wants you to understand that what happened had to happen and that you mustn't blame yourself. There are reasons for things. But you know that. I'll read it to you. I think it will help. When you get back, I'll give you a copy." I was astounded. I said that I could hardly believe that she was calling me with a poem at just the moment that I pleaded for help. Here is what she read:

Soul's Journey
Blessed is the mother earth
Great fortune has dawned upon her
The sun smiles gently and bursts brilliantly
over the mighty oceans, the roaring rivers,
the peaceful lakes, the flowing creeks and the gentle ponds.
The emerald world is blanketed in light that greets us
with all the treasures it holds,
like a baby in mother's arms,
The carpeted dunes sing out in joy
rippling sand in rhythm,
Rocky mountains loom in awe
shocking, alluring, mysterious,
Flowers bloom in rainbow colors,
swaying in the wind with ecstasy,
Fragrant, meditative memory of God,
Singing, dancing, leaping joyfully
the Universe is immersed in Grace
A soul is born
to reach for enlightenment
aiming at the truth,
Drenched in the nectar of life
with a taste for pain and pleasure alike,
Go above and beyond
and merge with the divine.[3]

I made it to New Jersey. Finally after thirty years, I
would hold my daughter in my arms. As she walked
through the door and down the hallway she said, "Mom?" I
said, "It's me." We fell into each other's arms and sobbed
for thirty minutes straight, unable to speak. We were
reunited as mother and daughter. She told me she had
always felt me with her on a spiritual level and had always
loved me. We were deeply connected. This reunion healed
places in me I didn't even know needed healing. To this
day, this healing continues for both Cindy and me.

3By Aditi Thatte and used by her permission.

I understood with all that needed to happen in the years that followed my experience of Self-Realization, it wasn't any wonder that I could not have remained in that state in July 1988. So much needed to be resolved. So much needed to be revealed and healed. These were not little things. Karma was such a mystery in the way it needed to be worked out. No wonder the spiritual masters have asked us to have compassion for ourselves and others.

Chapter 22

THE HEART ATTACK

So many years passed. It was now July 30, 2006. I had made many attempts to write this book, but life kept getting busier. Over the years, I had moved a few times and also became a serious student of homeopathy, a nature-based system of medicine. I had been practicing and teaching homeopathy as well as reiki and massage. Life was good and finally, I felt positioned to increase my income. I had just moved into a new apartment after living with my daughter, Deborah and grandson, Nicolas for the past three years. My daughter was about to get remarried to a wonderful man. My grandson was now six years old.

It was a warm and sunny Sunday afternoon and I decided to take my grandson to a nearby lake just four minutes from his house. We had lunch on the beach and swam in the lake. At some point, I began to feel a pain in my upper back which kept getting worse. Having been a fairly healthy person, I started to become worried. I decided I had better get help and called my daughter, as I wanted her to come and get Nicolas. I had Nicolas sit next to me as I called Deborah on my cell phone, telling her I thought I should go to the hospital. I have never said such a thing to my daughter, so she knew something was very wrong. I hung up from her and dialed 911. What I didn't know was my daughter immediately called our neighbor and friend, Ben. He was a paramedic. Ben happened to be home for the first time in two weeks. Then my daughter called 911. Both he and my daughter rushed to the lake in separate cars. She got there first and saw a policeman trying to set up some oxygen. Ben arrived within moments, then the ambulance. I was too sick to notice anyone.

On the way to the beach, Ben called the paramedic ambulance and the hospital where he knew I needed to go to for the proper medical care. Ben knew instinctively what I didn't know—that I was having a heart attack. I was later told by my cardiologist that if Ben had not been there, I would have been taken to a nearby hospital that did not have the special care I needed and I would have died. But fate and destiny were on my side, and God's angels in the form of doctors, paramedics, nurses, my daughter and my grandson were with me that day. I realized if my grandson were not with me, I would not have called my daughter first. If I had not called my daughter first, then Ben would not have been called.

Within moments I was loaded into the ambulance with Ben by my side. As I lay on the gurney, Ben looked in my eyes and said, "Don't worry, Mary, I won't let you go." He said that with so much conviction, that I felt completely safe and just let myself relax. A woman paramedic appeared in Ben's place and he said she would take good care of me. Ben went to the front of the ambulance to drive. The woman's face shone with grace and kindness. Clearly she loved her job. "She's God in action," I thought. There wasn't a moment to spare. I felt so ill, but still I didn't realize I was having a heart attack. Very quickly, I felt I was losing consciousness. I closed my eyes. A familiar window of Light appeared and instantly I felt calm. I knew it was God. I no longer felt my body, I no longer heard any sounds and I let myself completely rest in the Light. I then lost all consciousness.

I arrived at the hospital still unconscious and as Ben opened the door of the ambulance to take me out, I went into cardiac arrest. Instantly Ben brought me back to life using cardiac resuscitation. I was whisked into the cardiac catheterization unit where I received three stents. I was still unconscious and in critical condition. After they stabilized me, I was taken to a nearby larger hospital where I could have a bypass if needed. After arriving there, I received two more stents as I was too ill to have a bypass. Unfortunately, I also suffered a femoral bleed from the procedure of placing in the stents and needed seven pints of blood along with vascular surgery to repair the hole in my femoral artery. Miraculously, I survived. The doctors were amazed and my poor family members, who had been through so much, were grateful to everyone who attended me with so much grace, kindness and skill.

I had had the heart attack on Sunday and was unconscious until Wednesday. While unconscious, I had absolutely no awareness of anything, no light, no sound. I think I was in God's waiting room to see if I would stay or go. When I awoke, I was stunned to know all that had happened. I had no previous symptoms of a heart attack other than a sore feeling in my throat a few days beforehand. Many family members had arrived not only to see me, but for my daughter's wedding which was to take place that Saturday. I truly felt their loving presence made all the difference in my ability to survive.

One of the first things I noticed when I started to become conscious, was a lighter feeling in my heart. What was it? I realized by some divine intervention a lot of old suffering I was carrying around in my heart was gone. This was astonishing to me. How could that happen? It was gone and has not returned since. Although my heart felt so much lighter, physically I felt very weak. It took many days resting in the hospital and many days resting at home before I could regain any kind of energy. That gave me a lot of time to think.

Since I could not go back to my work and needed many

months of recuperation, I decided it must be time for me to finish writing this book. So many times before I tried to complete it, only to set it aside for many more years. But not now.

I was told by the doctors that most people never survive the kind of massive heart attack I had; Ben called it "The Widow Maker." I realized what a miracle it was for me to be alive: I realized that I must have been saved for a reason. Now, unable to do any of my familiar work, I knew writing this book *was* my work and I must finish it.

Chapter 23

HUMANITY EMERGING

As humanity emerges from the deep sleep of ignorance of its true Divine nature, the wisdom and knowledge contained within will emerge. A renaissance of the spirit will unfold. Quite naturally this new understanding will be reflected in all areas of study and human experience including medicine and nature, as well as death and dying.

Medicine and Nature

With the new understanding and experience of the reality of God-consciousness as the life force in the human body, vibrational medicine will be revisited with new eyes and a new comprehension. Homeopathy, as a vibrational and natural system of medicine, will reemerge in the 21st century as the preeminent system of preventive and curative medicine and will regain its popularity in the United States. Homeopathic medicine has a long history of success in every kind of epidemic and can even replace the need for the questionable and dangerous practice of vaccination; the theory behind vaccination will come under greater scrutiny. For me, the most astonishing power of homeopathy rests in its ability to prevent inherited traits from being passed down by parents to their children, which I call vibrational genetics. Much will be said about this in the future.

Western medicine will continue to prevail as the premiere system of medicine for life-threatening trauma and needed surgery. However, the use of chemical drugs with their harmful side effects in suppressing symptoms will diminish in favor of homeopathic remedies and their powerful ability to cure almost every conceivable acute and chronic ailment without side effects. This includes and is not limited to infections, allergies, flu, eczema, colds, epidemics, gastrointestinal and circulatory problems, as well as depression, anxiety and behavioral issues. Homeopathic prescribing is based on the individual's symptom picture which includes the mental/emotional state.

My most recent experience in the hospital provides an example of homeopathy's power to cure acute infections. As I had mentioned in the previous chapter, I had a severe heart attack requiring cardiac resuscitation, five stents and vascular surgery. Needless to say, my whole being experienced extreme trauma. I had tubes and intravenous in my body including a tube in my bladder. After the bladder tube was removed, I experienced many subsequent days of blood tests and needle sticks. Then after a brief and very traumatic few days at a less than desirable rehabilitation hospital, I was readmitted back to the cardiac hospital. Many more tests were performed.

After readmission to the cardiac hospital, I started having symptoms of a bladder infection, a first in my life. I knew that in Western medicine antibiotics would be prescribed to suppress the symptoms of the bladder infection with the idea that the bacteria found in my urine was the culprit. With my homeopathic training I knew the culprit was the extreme trauma I had suffered affecting my body and soul, compromising my immune system. The precipitating events were the physical and emotional trauma, including the bladder tube. But what finally tipped the balance many days after the bladder tube had been removed, was the emotional trauma I suffered at the brief stay at the rehabilitation hospital. Due to my weakened condition, feeling trapped in that horrid place, I felt like a helpless victim. My whole being felt assaulted. As a result, my immune system became weak, allowing an imbalance of bacterial growth. Now safely back at the cardiac hospital, I knew exactly what I needed. I knew I needed to remove the trauma from my whole being which included my emotions, my mind and my physical body. Then my immune system would regain its strength and the bacterial balance in my body would naturally be restored. With mind and body in harmony, and my vital force restored, the symptoms of the bladder infection would simply disappear.

I knew the remedy I needed was staphasagria, at a high potency to match the strength of the trauma I experienced. Staphasagria is a remedy from nature, from the delphinium flower. Every homeopathic remedy has mental/emotional properties with certain affinities to various systems of the body. Staphasagria is a remedy of choice for the experience of being emotionally and/or physically assaulted as well as having an affinity for the urinary tract. Until I could have access to the remedy, I took two doses of an antibiotic knowing full well that it was not going to address my real problem. Although the antibiotic took the edge off the bladder discomfort, it didn't cure the discomfort, nor did I feel better from the trauma.

Finally, on the evening of the second day, a friend of mine brought the homeopathic remedy, a pellet of which I immediately put in a water bottle. Taking a teaspoon from the bottle every hour, after succussing the bottle before each dose (hitting the bottom of the bottle to increase the strength of each dose), the remedy brought immediate relief on every level. Within moments of taking the first dose, I felt an immediate sigh of relief in my whole being. First, I felt better on a mental and emotional level with a sense of well-being and then the relief of the bladder discomfort followed within thirty minutes. I took no further antibiotics. Within two days of taking the remedy, I was totally cured. My whole physical and emotional body felt much less traumatized and my energy was much better. Homeopathy once again proved its value as the premiere system of body/mind medicine.

I was trained as a registered nurse and served in Western medicine for eleven years and I was trained as a homeopath for the last eight years. I appreciate the roles of both Western and homeopathic medicine. I know these two systems of medicine can live harmoniously together in the world. Each has a rightful place.

For me, the study of homeopathy demystified disease. Homeopathy gave me a greater understanding of myself and the inter-relationship of my mental/emotional state and life circumstances and how they related to my physical expression of these. It further gave me the power to do something about it using preventive and curative methods.

The rebirth of homeopathy will come from the rebirth of the consciousness of mankind. When man knows who he is and his proper place as Divinity in human form, he will come to know what nature is, Divinity in plant form. With right understanding, right living, right thinking and right relationship with nature, most all diseases will disappear using remedies from nature in concert with our vital force, our consciousness.

In homeopathic philosophy it is said that there is no such thing as disease, only disharmony. To take it a step further, a friend of mind, who has experienced homeopathy, noted that there is no such thing as disharmony only disunion. This knowledge is already present within us, it is just a matter of accessing it. Here is a poem I wrote out of my experience over the last eight years using homeopathy for my family, friends and myself:

Sweet Companions
A leaf holds out its hand
to humanity and says,

"Enter the way of nature,
for in this Divine expression
rests the greatest mysteries:
soothing balms so that
man may not suffer."

In this Divine interplay
between nature and man
Bliss is known,

Gratitude cultivated
on one knee, as
humanity replies
plucking a leaf.

Union attained in measure
to a heart revealed
In the sweetest of companions:
Man and Nature.

There is a wonderful book with a great introduction to homeopathy that I wholeheartedly recommend. It was written by a computer scientist whose three year old son was cured of autism using homeopathy. The title is: "Impossible Cure, The Promise of Homeopathy" by Amy L. Lansky, PhD. Another book recounts the history of homeopathy in the United States and Great Britain: "The Faces of Homeopathy: an Illustrated History of the First 200 years" by Julian Winston. In this book, it is amazing to read about the many homeopathic schools of medicine, clinics, hospitals and homeopathic medical doctors successfully practicing in the United States at the turn of the last century.

Death and Dying

I know from my own death experience that as we connect with our God-consciousness, the fear of death and dying will disappear. I have read stories of Self-Realized beings who were conscious that they were about to leave their bodies.

They would let those around them know this was about to happen and then they would sit for meditation and leave. That is what happened to me that day I sat for meditation in the lobby of MIT. The only difference was that I had to return to my body, as it was not time for me to sever my bonds with the earth experience.

Meditation is a way for us to get in touch with our indwelling God-consciousness, our very own Self. In doing so we can travel to the inner realms of spirituality and connect with that inner core of peace and all-knowing. As we practice traveling in these inner realms, we can experience that death does not really exist and that we are eternal and immortal. When that happens, the fear of death will drop away. It is a very natural process. How and when we pass from this side to the other side will become a conscious process instead of a frightful experience.

Renaissance of the Spirit

A true renaissance of the Spirit is occurring. It will be reflected in the way we perform our work in the world and in the way we treat others. When we experience our Divinity within as a real and present Truth, it will become impossible to do injury to any living thing, including the living organism we call Mother Earth. We will have gained true Self-respect and the Divine love we have within will automatically flow out to others. Our educational, medical, environmental, financial, social and political systems will change for the better in the wake of this inner knowledge, as they will become a reflection of this inner Truth.

We are the ones ushering in this great turning towards enlightenment, the great renaissance of the Spirit. We are the ones invoking our very own Divinity to come to the forefront on the global stage. We are here giving birth to ourselves, whether we are very conscious of it or we are just beginning to feel an inner stirring. Never before has such an awakening to the God within each person ever occurred on such a global level in the hearts of humanity.

The most generous and socially kind act anyone can

perform is to experience and embrace their own great Self living in them as Divine consciousness here and now. Divinity stands within us waiting to be revealed. We only need to have the courage to open the door to the Divine Truth that lives inside.

I wrote the following poem as an expression of the commonality of our experiences and challenges and the common bonds we share:

Together
We share the same stories,
We share the same pain.
We cry for our families,
Our plights are the same.

We think we are different,
But if Truth would be known,
We share the same families,
This earth is our home.

In love we must travel,
Each one as a friend,
Till Light fills our hearts
and we reach journey's end.

For we are no different,
There's no yours or mine,
In Truth we are One,
Now, and for all Time.

May we emerge together from the identification of ourselves as mere ego-mind-personalities into the clear and present experience of the Truth of ourselves as God, right here in this moment. Everyone is included, everyone belongs, everyone is important, everyone is God. May we emerge together, triumphant!

Acknowledgments

First and foremost, I want to thank my spiritual teacher, who for the last twenty years has guided me and continues to guide me to Self-Realization. Such teachers are rare and it has been my great, good fortune to be in the company of one who has made the journey.

I also want to thank all the saints and great ones from all religions and all spiritual paths who are shining examples of the Light of God within beckoning us to take the inner adventure to discover the same Truth within: God.

On this earthly journey I want to especially thank my daughters, Deborah and Cindy who inspire me and make me so proud of the wonderful people and mothers they have become. Thanks and love to my grandchildren, who are full of life and make me laugh; they are such a blessing to this world. To my other family members, my newest son-in-law Ibar, siblings, relatives and to my dear parents, George and Mary who have passed into the Light, my heartfelt thanks for your love, support and companionship.

Thanks goes to all of those wonderful friends in my life who have supported me in body and soul in various roles along the way. They include Janice Cummings, India Hoeschen-Stein, Sheryl Dinisco, Edith Griffin, Karen Short, Nancy Strisik, Aditi Thatte, Donna Galloway and Liz Podsiadlo. My heartfelt thanks also goes to all my friends at my meditation center who have offered their prayers and support in every way for my benefit, especially during my recent health challenge.

A special thanks is offered to those who saved my life on the day of my near-fatal heart attack. Miracles happen and on that fateful day in July, 2006, a miracle happened to me.

To Ben Podsiadlo, my neighbor and family friend, who was my paramedic that day and performed cardiac pulmonary resuscitation which kept me alive. He also skillfully organized all the personnel who had an active roll in saving my life. I give him my unending gratitude and love. Our two families became one that day. To all the paramedics and to the doctors and nurses and all the hospital staff, thank you for your dedication and skill delivered with so much care and love. May God bless you in your service to humanity.

My great appreciation goes to all the teachers in my life who have enlightened me along the way with their knowledge in the fields of medicine, nursing, bodywork, reiki and in particular, homeopathy, the crown jewel of my healing journey. Homeopathy deserves a special mention because it has so profoundly transformed my understanding of disease and true healing on the deepest level.

Lastly, I want to thank my good friend, Joanne Shapiro, who has stood by me all the way in bringing this book to its publication. She has been with me as an editor and friend offering suggestions and spiritual support alike in fulfilling my life-long goal in the publication of this book. She stood by my family and me in my health crisis offering her love and support. Such friends are like gold. I also want to thank Kay Stoner who arrived at the perfect time to offer invaluable publishing suggestions and advice.

About the Author

Photo by Joanne Shapiro

Mary Terhune has been a health care practitioner for the past forty years. She began her practice in the healing arts as a registered nurse. After eleven years of practicing in Western medicine, she discovered alternative medicine out of a need to heal herself. She spent the next twenty years as a certified massage therapist and reiki master. She studied at the Renaissance Institute of Classical Homeopathy and has been studying, practicing and teaching classical homeopathy for the past seven years. She is a meditation practitioner and has been studying Eastern philosophy for the past twenty years. Mary has traveled to India and has a Self-Realized meditation master as her guide to the inner knowledge of Self-Realization. After suffering a near-fatal heart attack in July 2006, Mary went on sabbatical to recuperate and finish writing this book. In the near future, she will be offering talks on topics included in the book. Her website is: www.ournaturaldestiny.com and she can be reached at ournaturaldestiny@yahoo.com.